DECOYING THE YANKS

Jackson's Valley Campaign

ACTION IN THE SHENANDOAH, JANUARY–JUNE 1862

As the Union's troops marched on Richmond in the spring of 1862, Confederate forces under General Thomas Jonathan "Stonewall" Jackson staged a strategic diversion west of the Blue Ridge Mountains in the Shenandoah Valley. After a winter advance on Romney, Jackson's army marched nearly the length of the Valley two times in less than a month, fighting a string of battles (*crossed swords*) on a route that stretched from McDowell in the Allegheny Mountains to Harpers Ferry on the Potomac River. Using speed and a superior knowledge of the terrain, Jackson eluded three Federal commands assigned to destroy his outnumbered forces. And, by posing a threat to Washington, Jackson distracted the Federals from their primary objective — the capture of Richmond — and drew off thousands of Federal troops that would have joined the advance on the Confederate capital.

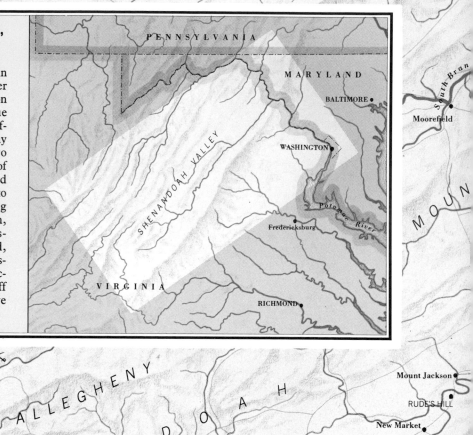

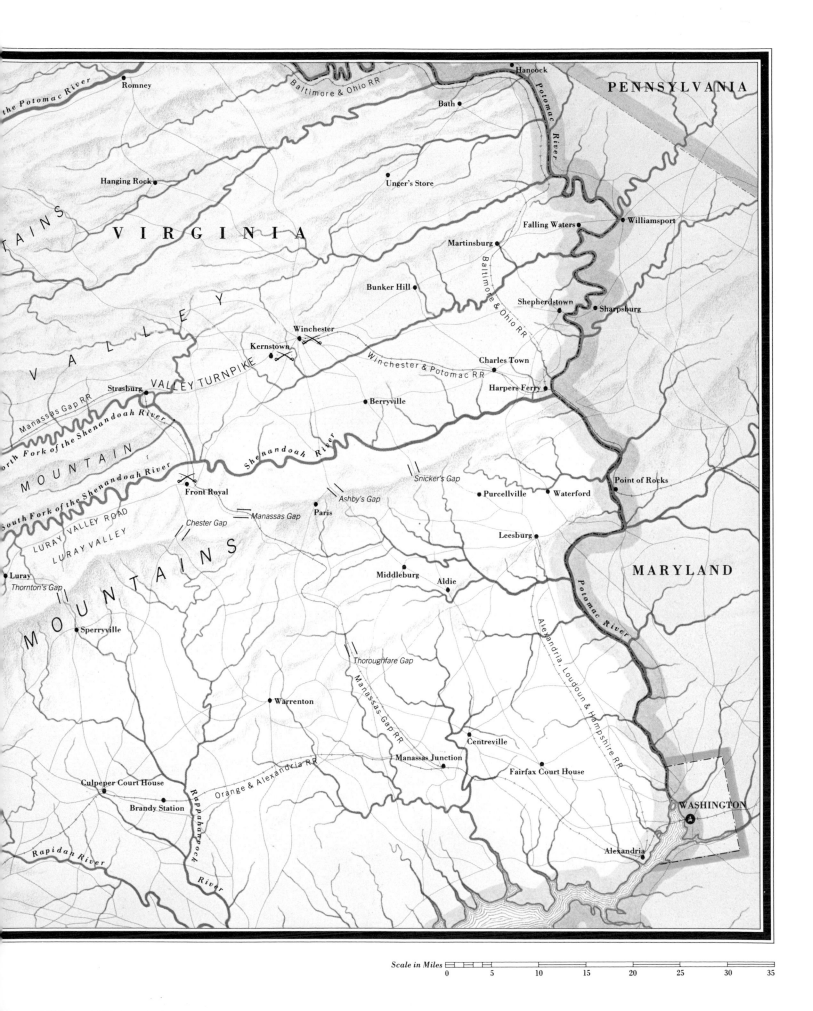

PENNSYLVANIA

the Potomac River

Romney

Baltimore & Ohio RR

Hancock

Bath

Potomac River

V I R G I N I A

Unger's Store

Hanging Rock

Falling Waters

Williamsport

Martinsburg

V A L L E Y

Bunker Hill

Baltimore & Ohio RR

Shepherdstown

Sharpsburg

Winchester

Kernstown

Charles Town

Winchester & Potomac RR

Strasburg

VALLEY TURNPIKE

Harpers Ferry

Manassas Gap RR

Berryville

North Fork of the Shenandoah River

Shenandoah River

M O U N T A I N

South Fork of the Shenandoah River

Snicker's Gap

Point of Rocks

Front Royal

Ashby's Gap

Purcellville

Waterford

Manassas Gap

Paris

Luray Valley Road

Chester Gap

Leesburg

Luray Valley

M O U N T A I N S

MARYLAND

Luray

Thornton's Gap

Middleburg

Aldie

Potomac River

M O U N T A I N S

Sperryville

Alexandria, Loudoun & Hampshire RR

Thoroughfare Gap

Manassas Gap RR

Warrenton

Centreville

Manassas Junction

Fairfax Court House

Culpeper Court House

Orange & Alexandria RR

Rappahannock River

WASHINGTON

Brandy Station

Rapidan River

Alexandria

River

Scale in Miles

0   5   10   15   20   25   30   35

Other Publications:

PLANET EARTH
COLLECTOR'S LIBRARY OF THE CIVIL WAR
LIBRARY OF HEALTH
CLASSICS OF THE OLD WEST
THE EPIC OF FLIGHT
THE GOOD COOK
THE SEAFARERS
WORLD WAR II
HOME REPAIR AND IMPROVEMENT
THE OLD WEST
LIFE LIBRARY OF PHOTOGRAPHY (revised)
LIFE SCIENCE LIBRARY (revised)

For information on and a full description of any of the
Time-Life Books series listed above, please write:
Reader Information, Time-Life Books
541 North Fairbanks Court, Chicago, Illinois 60611

This volume is one of a series that chronicles in full the
events of the American Civil War, 1861-1865.
Other books in the series include:
Brother against Brother: The War Begins
First Blood: Fort Sumter to Bull Run
The Blockade: Runners and Raiders
The Road to Shiloh: Early Battles in the West
Forward to Richmond: McClellan's Peninsular Campaign

The Cover: Confederate Major General Richard
Ewell (*center*) and Brigadier General Turner Ashby
(*right*) confer with their commander, Thomas J.
"Stonewall" Jackson, atop a ridge overlooking the
Shenandoah Valley. During the spring of 1862,
Jackson waged a brilliant campaign in the Valley to
lure Federal forces away from Richmond.

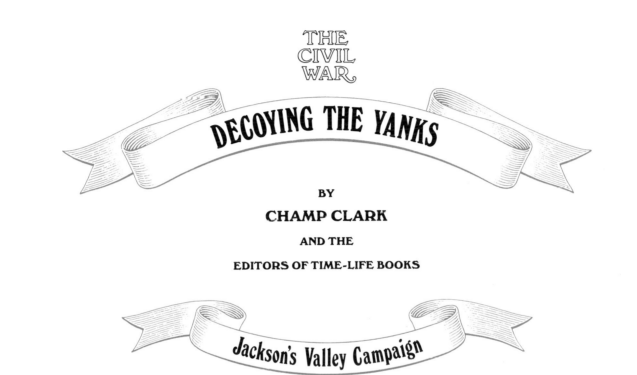

THE CIVIL WAR

DECOYING THE YANKS

BY

CHAMP CLARK

AND THE

EDITORS OF TIME-LIFE BOOKS

Jackson's Valley Campaign

TIME-LIFE BOOKS, ALEXANDRIA, VIRGINIA

Time-Life Books Inc.
is a wholly owned subsidiary of

TIME INCORPORATED

FOUNDER: Henry R. Luce 1898-1967

Editor-in-Chief: Henry Anatole Grunwald
President: J. Richard Munro
Chairman of the Board: Ralph P. Davidson
Executive Vice President: Clifford J. Grum
Editorial Director: Ralph Graves
Group Vice President, Books: Joan D. Manley

TIME-LIFE BOOKS INC.

EDITOR: George Constable
Executive Editor: George Daniels
Director of Design: Louis Klein
Board of Editors: Dale M. Brown,
Thomas A. Lewis, Robert G. Mason,
Ellen Phillips, Gerry Schremp, Gerald Simons,
Rosalind Stubenberg, Kit van Tulleken
Director of Administration: David L. Harrison
Director of Research: Carolyn L. Sackett
Director of Photography: John Conrad Weiser

PRESIDENT: Reginald K. Brack Jr.
Senior Vice President: William Henry
Vice Presidents: George Artandi, Stephen L. Bair,
Peter G. Barnes, Robert A. Ellis, Juanita T. James,
Christopher T. Linen, James L. Mercer,
Joanne A. Pello, Paul R. Stewart

The Civil War
Editors: Gerald Simons, Henry Woodhead
Designer: Herbert H. Quarmby
Chief Researcher: Philip Brandt George

Editorial Staff for *Decoying the Yanks*
Associate Editors: John Newton (text);
Jane N. Coughran (pictures)
Staff Writers: William C. Banks, Allan Fallow,
Adrienne George, David Johnson, Glenn McNatt,
Peter Pocock
Researchers: Kristin Baker, Susan V. Kelly (principals);
Harris J. Andrews, Pat Good, Gwen C. Mullen,
Brian C. Pohanka
Assistant Designer: Cynthia T. Richardson
Copy Coordinator: Stephen G. Hyslop
Picture Coordinator: Donna Quaresima
Editorial Assistant: Andrea E. Reynolds

Editorial Operations
Design: Anne B. Landry (art coordinator); James J. Cox
(quality control)
Research: Phyllis K. Wise (assistant director),
Louise D. Forstall
Copy Room: Diane Ullius (director), Celia Beattie
Production: Gordon E. Buck, Peter Inchauteguiz

Correspondents: Elisabeth Kraemer (Bonn); Margot
Hapgood, Dorothy Bacon (London); Miriam Hsia, Lucy
T. Voulgaris (New York); Maria Vincenza Aloisi,
Josephine du Brusle (Paris); Ann Natanson (Rome).
Valuable assistance was also provided by: Mirka
Gondicas (Athens); Carolyn Chubet (New York).

The Author:
Champ Clark, a veteran of 23 years as a correspondent,
writer and senior editor for *Time*, retired from weekly
journalism in 1972 in order to freelance and teach in the
English Department at the University of Virginia. He
is the author of *The Badlands* in the Time-Life Books
series The American Wilderness, and of *Flood* in the
Planet Earth series.

The Consultants:
Colonel John R. Elting, USA (Ret.), a former Associate
Professor at West Point, is the author of *Battles for Scandi-
navia* in the Time-Life Books World War II series and of
*The Battle of Bunker's Hill, The Battles of Saratoga, Mili-
tary History and Atlas of the Napoleonic Wars* and *American
Army Life*. He is also editor of the three volumes of *Military Uniforms in America, 1755-1867*, and associate editor
of *The West Point Atlas of American Wars*.

James I. Robertson Jr. is C. P. Miles Professor of History
at Virginia Tech. The recipient of the Nevins-Freeman
Award and other prizes in the field of Civil War history,
he has written or edited some 20 books, which include *The
Stonewall Brigade, Civil War Books: A Critical Bibliography* and *Civil War Sites in Virginia*.

William A. Frassanito, a Civil War historian and lecturer
specializing in photograph analysis, is the author of two
award-winning studies, *Gettysburg: A Journey in Time* and
*Antietam: The Photographic Legacy of America's Bloodiest
Day*, and a companion volume, *Grant and Lee, The Virginia Campaigns*. He has also served as chief consultant to the
photographic history series *The Image of War*.

Les Jenson, Curator of the U.S. Army Transportation
Museum at Fort Eustis, Virginia, specializes in Civil War
artifacts and is a conservator of historic flags. He is a
contributor to *The Image of War* series, a freelance writer
and consultant for numerous Civil War publications and
museums, and a member of the Company of Military Historians. He was formerly Curator of the Museum of the
Confederacy in Richmond, Virginia.

Michael McAfee specializes in military uniforms and has
been Curator of Uniforms and History at the West Point
Museum since 1970. A fellow of the Company of Military
Historians, he coedited with Colonel John Elting *Long
Endure: The Civil War Years*, and he collaborated with
Frederick Todd on *American Military Equipage*. He has
written numerous articles for *Military Images Magazine*,
as well as *Artillery of the American Revolution, 1775-1783*.

Library of Congress Cataloguing in Publication Data
Clark, Champ.
  Decoying the yanks.
  (The Civil War)
  Bibliography: p.
  Includes index.
  1. Shenandoah Valley Campaign, 1861. 2. Shenandoah
Valley Campaign, 1862. 3. Jackson, Stonewall, 1824-
1863. I. Time-Life Books. II. Title. III. Series.
E472.6.C58 1984   973.7'31   83-9138
ISBN 0-8094-4724-X
ISBN 0-8094-4725-8 (lib. bdg.)

CONTENTS

Imperiled Land of Milk and Honey

"Everything had a thrifty look," wrote a Confederate soldier in the Shenandoah Valley in 1861. "The horses and cattle were fat and sleek; the large barns were overflowing with the gathered crops; the houses looked comfortable; and the fences were in splendid order. It was truly a land of milk and honey."

Nature had indeed been kind to this verdant strip of land between the Blue Ridge and the Allegheny Mountains. Its hot springs and magnificent scenery attracted travelers from as far away as Europe. Among the visitors was Edward Beyer, a German landscapist whose paintings on these pages portray the Shenandoah Valley's prewar mood of pastoral tranquillity.

The Indians who lived in the Valley called it "Daughter of the Stars." And the prosperous settlers, many of them pacifist Mennonites and Dunkers from Pennsylvania and Maryland, considered themselves blessed.

These quiet, religious people worked

In this panoramic view of the Shenandoah Valley as seen from Rockfish Gap in the Blue Ridge Mountains, two horseback riders wend their way to the Mountain House,

diligently to improve their land. They crushed Valley limestone to build macadam roads and harnessed streams and rivers to generate power for machine shops, foundries, and textile and flour mills. Fields in the Valley produced wheat at nearly double the yields of farmland elsewhere in Virginia. There were no great plantations and few slaves, no conspicuously wealthy families and little poverty. The settlers of the Shenandoah Valley felt that theirs was a world apart, boundless in potential and stimulating to the human spirit.

The advent of the Civil War threatened to shatter this special world between the mountain barriers. The Shenandoah's strategic location and sheer abundance made it a military objective for both sides. Not only was the Valley a natural corridor between North and South, but its fields could feed armies. Forage was everywhere.

Soon the sound of cannon would echo from ridge to ridge as the Valley became a giant battlefield. "As the superb scenery opened before us," a Federal soldier wrote, "there was no foreshadowing of the terror, the desolation and death that were to follow."

a resort on the Staunton-Charlottesville Road. In the background, a Virginia Central train chugs toward the towering Alleghenies on the horizon.

A health spa *(center)* dominates the town of Warm Springs, a county seat in the central Valley. The resort was a popular watering place for the residents of Richmond.

Beneath twin mountains called the Peaks of Otter, near the village of Liberty, fat dairy cattle graze contentedly in a lush pasture as farmers take in a hay crop. At the edge

of the field, a train steams along the Virginia & Tennessee Railroad, which connects the Valley with Richmond to the east and Memphis to the west.

A series of cascades called Falling Springs drop from a towering cliff at the headwaters of the James River.

Bearing torches to light the way, tourists explore the spectacular formations in Weyer's Cave, north of Staunton.

A 93-foot-long limestone arch called Natural Bridge spans Cedar Creek in the Shenandoah Valley south of Lexington.

The U.S. Armory established by George Washington at Harpers Ferry stretches along the bank at the confluence of the Shenandoah and Potomac Rivers. At center

is a railroad bridge on the Baltimore & Ohio line, an important rail link between Washington and the West.

Into the Valley

"General Lee was the handsomest man I ever saw. John C. Breckinridge was a model of manly beauty, John B. Gordon, a picture for the sculptor, and Joe Johnston looked every inch a soldier. None of these things could be said of Jackson."

LIEUTENANT HENRY KYD DOUGLAS, AIDE TO GENERAL THOMAS J. JACKSON

1

The 1st Virginia Brigade, encamped on a farm not far from the stream called Bull Run, lined up in close column on the morning of November 4, 1861. The 1,800 men present snapped to attention and stood waiting for long moments. Nothing moved but their bullet-torn battle flags, stirring a little in the light breeze.

Then into the grassy clearing ambled a small, scruffy sorrel horse of dubious pedigree and uncertain gait, carrying a rider whose disreputable appearance belied his only adornments — the stars and wreath of a general. His coat was a faded relic from the Mexican War era. The visor of his shapeless cap was pulled far down, shadowing the grim, bearded face and concealing the blue eyes that took on a feverish glitter in the frenzy of battle. He sat his horse awkwardly, torso bent forward as if leaning into a stiff wind, legs akimbo in flop-top boots, and gigantic feet (estimated at size 14 although he was only 5 feet 10 inches tall) thrust into shortened stirrups.

The general reined the little horse to a halt and prepared to address the silent ranks. He disliked speaking before large groups and was poor at it. For a decade before the War he had lectured as a professor of Natural and Experimental Philosophy and as an instructor of Artillery Tactics at the Virginia Military Institute. His classes had been notorious for their sedative quality. He had once been overwhelmed by embarrassment when, as a deacon of his Presbyterian church in Lexington, he had been called upon to lead prayers. Yet as he addressed the brigade that bore his nickname, Stonewall, he spoke with a certain stiff eloquence.

"Officers and men of the First Brigade," he began in his high-pitched voice. "I am not here to make a speech but simply to say farewell. I first met you at Harpers Ferry in the commencement of the War, and I cannot take leave of you without giving expression to my admiration of your conduct from that day to this, whether on the march, in the bivouac, or on the bloody plains of Manassas. I shall look with great anxiety to your future movements, and I trust whenever I shall hear of the First Brigade on the field of battle it will be of still nobler deeds achieved and higher reputation won."

The general stopped as if done. Then, caught by a surge of emotion, he flung his reins on the sorrel's neck, rose in his stirrups and stretched out his right hand in the gesture of Joshua.

"In the Army of the Shenandoah," he cried, "you were the First Brigade; in the Army of the Potomac you were the First Brigade; in the Second Corps of this army you are the First Brigade; you are the First Brigade in the affections of your General; and I hope by your future deeds and bearing you will be handed down to posterity as the First Brigade in our second War of Independence.

"Farewell!"

Thomas Jonathan Jackson was a 31-year-old faculty member at the Virginia Military Institute in Lexington when this daguerreotype was made in 1855.

At Jackson's Mill, the Jackson family holdings near Weston in western Virginia, the orphaned Thomas spent the happiest years of his boyhood. Under the care of his uncle Cummins, young Jackson worked hard at farm chores, supervised slaves cutting timber and helped to operate the sawmill and gristmill.

Then Major General Thomas Jonathan Jackson wheeled Little Sorrel and, followed by wild yells from the men, started his journey to his new command in the great Shenandoah Valley of Virginia.

"If this Valley is lost," Jackson once insisted in a letter to a friend, "Virginia is lost." And it was widely believed that if Virginia were lost, the Confederacy would perish. Whatever the validity of these surmises, the Shenandoah was of vital strategic import to both sides, and politicians in Washington as well as Richmond were poignantly aware of that fact.

In Confederate hands, the Valley was a salient thrusting into the Union's eastern front; terminating on the Potomac 30 miles northwest of Washington, the Valley flanked the capital menacingly. So long as the Shenandoah Valley was controlled by Confederate forces, Federal authorities in Washington, Maryland and even Pennsylvania would remain restless and apprehensive of their security.

If the Valley were to fall into Federal hands, Confederate troops in the Piedmont region east of the Blue Ridge Mountains would stand in constant danger of attacks through the 11 passes from the Shenandoah. In the Valley's southern reaches, a Federal force in control of Staunton would threaten the crucial Virginia & Tennessee Railroad, which ran from Richmond to the Mississippi River. Indeed Richmond itself would be imperiled, and the cornucopia of foodstuffs produced in the Valley would be denied to the Confederacy.

Keeping the Shenandoah for the Confederacy and exploiting it as a threat to the Union would be Jackson's mission for the next eight months of his life. On the scale of campaigns in the Civil War, his Valley Campaign would be minuscule; his puny army would never number more than 17,000 men, and its few pitched battles taken together would not compare in size or casualties with such major clashes as Seven Pines or Shiloh. The campaign was basically a grueling series of maneuvers in which Jackson, driving his men until their feet bled, led the Federals on one wild-goose chase after another. In one period of 48 days on the march, his men covered 646 miles.

Yet for the very reason that it succeeded brilliantly without costly battles, the Valley Campaign enshrined Jackson as one of history's great captains. It demonstrated dramatically the powerful strategic influence that small armies, operating on the enemy's flank and threatening his rear, can exert on major theaters of war. The shattering blows delivered by Jackson in the sequestered Valley of the Shenandoah had the effect of temporarily paralyzing the 120,000 Federals McClellan was preparing to send against Richmond and eventually diverting 40,000 troops from the offensive. Thanks largely to this diversion, the Confederacy's vital communications center was saved, and the course of the great conflict prolonged.

These accomplishments astonished friend as well as foe, and all the more so because they were the work of an eccentric often dismissed as "Fool Tom."

Thomas J. Jackson was an unlikely combination of opposites. He was a tender husband who doted on children, but also a pitiless disciplinarian who "would have a man shot at the drop of a hat," remarked one of his soldiers, "and drop it himself." He worshipped a gentle God and taught Bible stories to a Sunday school class for slaves that he had himself founded in Lexington. But like Gideon he would raise a zealot's sword against the impious foe.

He was a lifelong hypochondriac, always seeking relief in peculiar diets, odd exercises and quack cures, but as a soldier he imperturbably endured the worst rigors of the field. In battle the dreary professor who repeated his textbook lessons by rote was replaced by an inspiring commander capable of guile and innovation. A self-effacing citizen at home, seemingly content to putter about in his garden, he was on the battlefield a savage fighter compelled to seek summits of glory. One of his officers, Brigadier General Richard Taylor, once caught a glimpse of Jackson's inner nature. "It was but a glimpse," he wrote. "Yet in that moment I saw an ambition boundless as Cromwell's, and as merciless."

Yet the conflicts and contradictions were only part of the essential man. To a large extent, Thomas Jackson was the logical product of his past.

He was born in 1824 in the mountain town of Clarksburg, on Virginia's western frontier, an area that would later give its allegiance to the Union. He came from respectable stock, the son of an amiable young lawyer with an unfortunate tendency to underwrite bad investments. The debt-ridden father had died of typhoid when Tom was two, leaving an impoverished widow who survived her husband by only five years. Tom, his older brother, Warren, and younger sister, Laura, were brought up by several different relatives.

Once, the boys ran away to visit their sister and then went skylarking on the Mississippi River for several months. Tom returned with a severe case of ague to show for his travels; the experience was one about which Jackson, always taciturn, was forever after especially reticent.

It was during his unsettled childhood that Jackson first began complaining of a mysterious stomach malady for which physicians, then or later, could find no organic explanation. Whether real or fancied, the dyspeptic condition in particular and his uncertain health in general became central concerns to Jackson for the rest of his life — and offer explanations for a number of his strangest habits.

For example, whether studying at West Point, calling with matrimonial intent upon suitable young ladies in Lexington (he had an affinity for preachers' daughters) or presiding over his military headquarters, Jackson always sat bolt upright, never allowing his spine to touch the back of his chair. The erect posture, he maintained, kept his internal organs in perfect alignment, preventing any compression that might bring on digestive miseries.

Inevitably, and following formulas of his own devising, Jackson became a devoted dietician, convinced among other things that pepper made his left leg itch. As a young officer, he wrote to his sister, Laura, urging upon her a breakfast of "stale wheat bread (not less than twenty-four hours old), fresh meat — broiled or roasted is best — the yolk of one or two eggs — the white is hardly worth eating as it requires digestion and affords but little nutrition." By the time he achieved fame as a commander in the Civil War, his menu was even more restricted, consisting primarily of plain bread or corn bread, raspberries, milk — and an endless

Jackson's Portable Chapel

Wherever Jackson went he took this prayer book and prayer table, along with the bell for summoning his troops to worship. At every encampment the general ordered tents pitched for chapel, and at the frequent religious services he even acted as usher for his men.

succession of lemons, which he sucked even in battle and whose source remains a minor historical mystery.

Observing their general, Jackson's men noted that he frequently raised one hand heavenward; they took the gesture to mean that he was consulting with his Maker. The real reason, as Jackson had explained to a friend years earlier, was much more mundane. His left arm, he solemnly said, was heavier than the right, and he lifted it so that "the blood would run back into his body and lighten it."

Jackson's health also seems to have been closely linked, at least in his own mind, to his religion. He was of course born and reared as a Christian, and he lived in an intensely Christian age, one in which strong men felt no embarrassment whatever at falling to their knees in prayer. Yet for much of his life Jackson had no formal church affiliation, and as late as his Mexican War service he admitted that he looked upon prayer and Bible study with "no feeling stronger than having performed a duty."

After the Mexican War, however, during a tour of duty at Fort Hamilton on Long Island, Jackson suffered through a period of bilious attacks so acute that he feared for his life. During his enfeeblement and recovery, he apparently sensed an affinity between God's wondrous ways and the physical condition of Thomas Jonathan Jackson. "My afflictions," he wrote his sister, "I believe were decreed by Heaven's Sovereign." And, later: "I believed that God would restore me to perfect health, and such continues to be my belief."

Although fervent to the point of fanaticism, Jackson was generally tolerant of the creeds and sinful frailties of others. He nei-

Jackson struggled to earn this diploma from West Point in 1846. Academically unprepared, he was lucky even to have gained an appointment; he was accepted only after the original appointee from his county found cadet life too spartan and resigned from the academy.

ther smoked, drank, cursed, danced, played cards nor attended theater, yet he displayed little reformist zeal. He refrained from playful pastimes, he once said, less because he was certain that they were wicked than because "I know it is not wrong *not to do*, so I'm going to be on the safe side."

This was the Jackson who became the tithing pillar of his Presbyterian church — and this was the Jackson who became a war leader. He had no particular difficulty in deciding when to render to Caesar and when to render to God. He strongly believed that Sunday should be set aside for worship, and he would not even write a letter on that day. But he reasoned that if the Lord in His Wisdom chose to place a vulnerable enemy in Jackson's path on the Sabbath, then His Will be done. During the Valley Campaign, Jackson would fight no fewer than three battles on Sunday.

Undistracted by frivolities, Jackson was capable of tremendous concentration. It was one of his greatest strengths, and he demonstrated it early. When he reported to West Point on June 20, 1842, under appointment through a Congressman who owed his family a political debt, Jackson was a shambling hillbilly with the equivalent of a fourth-grade education. Asked how he might conceivably hope to keep pace with more advanced cadets at West Point, Jackson replied, "I can make it up in study."

He accomplished just that — by doing very little else. Long after taps had sounded and other cadets were slumbering, Jackson was still at his books by the glow of a coal fire. He was silent and unsociable, but he hung on desperately for a semester and then slowly rose in his class rankings, graduating 17th in a class of 59. "No one I have ever known," recalled one of his roommates, "could so perfectly withdraw his mind from surrounding objects or influences, and so thoroughly involve his whole being in the subject under consideration."

Jackson worked for military laurels in the same grim, grinding way during the Mexican War. Upon receiving his second lieutenant's commission in 1846, he was assigned to the 1st Artillery Regiment and sent to Point Isabel, Texas, General Zachary Taylor's base of operations. Taylor had already taken Monterey, and Jackson feared that the War would soon be over. "I envy you men who have been in battle," he told Daniel Harvey Hill, a young officer who had seen action with Taylor. Then Jackson added wistfully: "How I should like to be in *one* battle."

Jackson got his wish and then some. At the siege of Vera Cruz he served with the most advanced batteries, which frequently came under devastating counterbombardment from the Mexicans. For "gallant and meritorious conduct" there, he was promoted to first lieutenant.

After the battle of Cerro Gordo, Jackson learned that Captain John Bankhead Magruder had been given command of a captured enemy battery of four guns. Magruder was now looking for officers to assist him; since he was known as a martinet, however, volunteers were lacking. Jackson eagerly seized the opportunity. "When I heard that John Magruder had got his battery," Jackson explained later, "I bent all my energies to be with him, for I knew if any fighting was to be done, Magruder would be 'on hand.'"

He was right about that. With Magruder, Jackson was in the thick of the American assaults on Churubusco, the castle of Chapultepec and the San Cosme gate to Mexico City. By the end of the War, he was a brevet major who had been publicly praised by none other than the commander of the invasion force, General Winfield Scott. Moreover, Jackson had learned in Mexico that his mind was at its clearest and his powers of decision at their greatest when the firing was hottest, and that his only fear was "lest I should not meet danger enough to make my conduct conspicuous."

Jackson cuts a dashing figure in a daguerreotype made in Mexico City in 1847. The 23-year-old artillery lieutenant spent nine pleasant months in the conquered city, studying Spanish, learning to dance and, by his own account, falling in love for the first time with a beautiful *señorita*.

Like most mortals of driving purpose, Jackson was convinced of his own infallible correctness; in his silent way he was thus exceedingly contentious, and his prickly relationships with his military superiors as well as his subordinates would mark his career — and frequently mar it. In war's hurly-burly he had got along well with the tempestuous Magruder. But in the relative tranquillity of a peacetime assignment, his tendencies toward disputation would soon emerge in an astonishing and obsessive petty controversy with another superior.

After his two-year stay at Fort Hamilton, Jackson in October of 1850 was ordered to Florida, where Seminole Indian renegades led by one Billy Bowlegs were from time to time raiding white settlements. At Fort Meade, a miasmic little outpost on the Peace River southeast of Tampa, Jackson came under the command of another Mexican War veteran, William Henry French. Although both men were brevet majors, French was senior in service and was therefore Jackson's superior.

An officer of aldermanic girth, French exuded bluff good humor; behind that façade, however, lay a nature jealous of prerogatives and unwilling to delegate responsibilities. French met his measure in Jackson, who

On the outskirts of Mexico City, Jackson's two-gun battery lays down supporting fire for cavalry attacking enemy troops at Chapultepec castle on September 13, 1847. Moments earlier, with one of the guns, Jackson and his sergeant had turned the tide of the battle by knocking out an enemy strongpoint that had blocked the entire American advance.

somehow concluded that he had almost autonomous authority in carrying out his duties as company quartermaster and commissary officer. Matters came to a head in an argument over who should control the labors of a single workman who was constructing new buildings on the post.

Before long, Jackson and French were no longer on sociable speaking terms, and on March 23, 1851, Jackson wrote to Florida Department headquarters, complaining that French had usurped his "rights over the construction of the buildings." French forwarded the protest with a note of his own, which scoffed at "the pretensions of Brevet Major Jackson."

The result was a rebuke to Jackson. Brevet Brigadier General Thomas Childs, commander of troops in Florida, ruled that Jackson's assertion of independence would, if sanctioned, "reverse an established military principle that the Senior Officer shall command & give all necessary orders." Childs added that a difference of opinion between officers "ought never to degenerate into personalities, or to be considered a just cause for withholding the common courtesies of life so essential in an Officer & to the happiness & quiet of garrison life."

That pronouncement should have been more than enough to lay the issue to rest. But neither Jackson nor French was willing to quit, and their continued hostilities took a toll on Jackson's health. Complaining of failing eyesight and other ailments, he reported sick and took to his tent. And from there, incredibly, he launched an investigation into camp gossip that his commanding officer was dallying with a household servant named Julia.

Jackson quizzed seven enlisted men and

got only inconclusive replies. But a sergeant soon reported his inquiries to French, who was understandably aggrieved and placed Jackson under arrest for "Conduct Unbecoming an Officer and a Gentleman." In turn Jackson set about preparing a list of about 20 countercharges and, pleading his ill health, audaciously asked French to assign an enlisted man to help him transcribe the accusations — a request that French, amazingly, granted. When the post surgeon intervened, arguing that French's wife was being made the real victim of the vendetta and urging Jackson to cease and desist, Jackson wept in sympathy — but insisted that his Christian "conscience compelled him to prosecute the case."

Goaded beyond endurance, French finally wrote Childs's superior, Brevet Major General David E. Twiggs, "in order that the truth may keep an even pace with so malicious a slander and falsehood." Julia, he explained, was "a respectable White woman who has lived in my family for nearly nine years. Has faithfully attended my wife and children in health and devotedly nursed them in sickness. I know of nothing which should or shall prevent me from appearing in public as in private what I am, and ought to be, her friend and her protector." Pressing his own charges against Jackson, he promised that "when Major Jackson is brought to trial for his outrageous conduct the evidence which I will bring before the court will cover him with the infamy he deserves."

By the time the disgraceful affair was ended, the war of words had reached all the way to Washington and the ample lap of the General in Chief of the United States Army, Winfield Scott — who bounced the whole matter back to General Twiggs. That officer, utterly fed up, impatiently ruled that French had "shown himself incapable of conducting the service harmoniously at a detached post" and ordered him transferred to another station in a subordinate role.

Although rebuked by General Scott, Jackson was allowed to remain at his post and escaped further official censure. Nevertheless, he seized upon an opportunity to resign from the U.S. Army in August 1851 and join the faculty of the Virginia Military Institute (VMI) in Lexington. His friend from Mexican War days, Daniel Harvey Hill, now a professor at neighboring Washington (later Washington and Lee) College, had helped arrange the appointment.

One of Jackson's first acts at VMI was to ask the cadet adjutant for a copy of the institute's regulations. On receiving it, Jackson declared, "This is our *chart.*"

He meant it. Professor Jackson's unbending adherence to the rulebook would be the bane of cadets beyond number, and student notebooks were replete with such scrawled grumblings as "Old Jack skinned me today I tell you he did," and "He will skin on anything."

Jackson could enforce regulations, but try as he might, he could not compel students to take an interest in his droned pedagogy. To most of the cadets he was "Fool Tom," and a fit subject for ridicule. Yet the situation had its serious side. On one occasion, Jackson's discourse was interrupted by chatter from a sector of the classroom where sat James A. Walker, one of the academy's brightest students and livelier spirits. Jackson at first pointed an accusing finger at another cadet, then settled on Walker as the culprit and placed him on report.

The unhappy incident led to a court mar-

tial in which Walker defended himself: "Either I did make noise, or I did not. When the noise was made Major Jackson accused Mr. Mason of making it. It is strange that he should accuse Mr. Mason of making noise if he did not think he made it; and it is stranger still that he should report me if he thought Mr. Mason made it."

Despite such inexorable logic, Walker was found guilty of insubordination and, only a few months before his scheduled graduation, expelled from VMI. Outraged, Walker challenged Jackson to a duel. Although there was only a slight chance that Jackson would accept — dueling was, after all, to him unchristian — VMI Superintendent Francis H. Smith was concerned to the extent of writing Walker's father about the youth: "I would advise you to come up at once and take him home as I have reason to believe he may involve himself in serious difficulty." James Walker left peaceably, but he and Jackson would meet again.

In Jackson's personal life, bliss and tragedy were mixed, with scarcely a step missed in his orderly routine. Only a few weeks before Jackson took up his post at VMI, a physician had prescribed marriage and buttermilk to settle his nervous stomach. Soon, following the doctor's prescription, Jackson was paying court to Miss Elinor Junkin, daughter of the Reverend Dr. George Junkin, President of Washington College. They were married, with Ellie's father officiating, on August 4, 1853. The union was "a great source of happiness," Jackson wrote to his sister, but after only 14 months Ellie was dead, along with their stillborn baby.

Jackson sought comfort in his Christian faith. His religion, he wrote his sister, "is all that I desire it to be. I am reconciled for my

The fortress-like Virginia Military Institute at Lexington in the Shenandoah Valley had 117 cadets from throughout the South when Jackson joined the faculty in 1851.

loss and have joy and hope of a future reunion where the wicked cease from troubling and the weary are at rest."

After a trip to Europe in the summer of 1856, Jackson returned filled with renewed matrimonial purpose. He began corresponding with Mary Anna Morrison, daughter of the Reverend Dr. Robert Hall Morrison, who had been the first President of Davidson College. Jackson had met Anna, as she was called, several years before, while she was visiting her sister, Mrs. Daniel Harvey Hill, in Lexington. Now, during the Christmas holidays, he arrived unannounced at Anna's North Carolina home and made it clear to a somewhat bemused Reverend Morrison that he sought his daughter's hand. By the time Jackson left, he and Anna were engaged, and he was shortly writing from Lexington to his betrothed: "And as my mind dwells on you, I love to give it a devotional turn, by thinking of you as a gift from our Heavenly Father."

They were married on July 16, 1857. Anna adored Jackson. Yet domiciling with him demanded an almost saintly tolerance for his daily schedule, which Anna described as "perfectly systematic."

He arose each morning at six and knelt in private prayer. A cold bath and a brisk walk, undertaken without regard for the weather, were followed at the stroke of seven by family prayers, which his servants were required to attend. "He never waited for any one," wrote Anna, "not even his wife."

After breakfast, Jackson went to VMI, where he taught from eight until eleven. Returning home, he studied — first his Bible and then his lessons for the next day. For this part of his regimen he stood — a posture that was presumably even less compressive of his

This unflattering sketch of Jackson and the derisive marginal comments were scrawled in an astronomy textbook by cadet Thomas B. Robinson of the Virginia Military Institute. Student complaints about Jackson became so persistent that the institute's alumni society was moved to question his teaching ability in a resolution to the school's board.

interior than sitting straight up — in front of a high desk especially made for the purpose. During this period, Anna said, "he would not permit any interruption."

Midday dinner came at one, followed dutifully by a half hour of conversation that, said Anna, "was one of the brightest periods in the home life." Afternoons were given over to working in his garden or on the 20-acre farm the Jacksons had bought near Lexington. In the evenings, more study. But this time, because his increasingly weak eyes now rebelled against the use of artificial light, Jackson sat with his face to the wall, "as silent and dumb as the sphinx," reviewing his lessons in his mind, without books. He firmly established that during this period he was not to be disturbed by any conversation. And then to bed.

All this came to an end on Sunday, the 21st of April, 1861, when Jackson received a message requiring him to lead a contingent of VMI cadets to Richmond, where they would act as drillmasters for Virginia recruits in the War that had just begun. The departure from Lexington was scheduled for 1 p.m., but Jackson gathered the cadets early for prayer service and kept them waiting in ranks until the precise minute, before shouting: "Right face! By file, left march!"

Major Thomas Jackson, at the age of 37, was off to war.

Within a week of his arrival in Richmond, Jackson was commissioned a colonel of Virginia Volunteers and named commander at Harpers Ferry, the old United States Arsenal town at the juncture of the Shenandoah and Potomac Rivers. There he found a gorgeous throng of generals and field officers, all with militia appointments, low on military knowledge but high on panoply, who were presumably instructing a volunteer force of about 4,500 in the rudiments of warfare. Recalled John D. Imboden, then an artillery captain and later a cavalry brigadier general: "The official display in Harpers Ferry of 'fuss and feathers' would have done no discredit to the Champs Élysées."

The showy nonsense was abruptly terminated by act of the Virginia General Assembly, which removed all militia officers above the rank of captain and made their posts available to gubernatorial appointees, of whom Jackson was one. "What a revolution three or four days had wrought!" wrote Imboden on his return from a brief visit to Richmond. In a small hotel room near the Harpers Ferry railroad bridge, Jackson and his adjutant "were at a little pine table figuring upon the rolls of the troops present. They were dressed in well-worn, dingy uniforms of professors in the Virginia Military Institute. The deposed officers had nearly all left for home or for Richmond in a high state of indignation."

Soon, Imboden continued, "the presence of a master mind was visible in the changed condition of the camp. Perfect order reigned everywhere. Instruction in the details of military duties occupied Jackson's whole time. He was the easiest man in our army to get along with pleasantly so long as one did his duty, but as inexorable as fate in exacting the performance of it." Colonel Jackson spent seven hours a day drilling his green troops and also found time for them to work fortifying the rugged hills that surrounded Harpers Ferry.

Here in Harpers Ferry, Jackson displayed a fetish for secrecy that was to become notorious. On his regular tour of outposts, he would put a finger to his lips and shake his head in silent admonition to local commanders against letting their men know of his presence. And when Anna Jackson became curious about her husband's activities, he wrote in gentle rebuke: "What do you want with military news? Don't you know that it is unmilitary and unlike an officer to write news respecting one's post? You wouldn't wish your husband to do an unofficer-like thing, would you?"

Though Jackson may have been excessively suspicious, the sensitive location of Harpers Ferry was reason enough to maintain secrecy. The town was situated on the main stem of the Baltimore & Ohio (B & O) Railroad, a vital line running between the Midwest and the East Coast. Thousands of tons of coal from Appalachian mines were

Jackson doted on both his first wife, Ellie (*left*), who died in 1854, and his second wife, Anna (*above*), who wrote of their happy marriage: "He luxuriated in the freedom of his home, and his joyfulness would have been incredible to those who saw him only when he put on his official dignity."

carried east daily along the double tracks. At Harpers Ferry the line crossed the Potomac River, leaving Virginia and entering the border state of Maryland on its way to Baltimore and Washington. Jackson was of course offended by the sight and sound of vital supplies on their way to the Federal troops in Washington, especially at night when he needed his sleep.

To complicate matters, however, the trains also transported goods for Maryland's large Southern-leaning civilian minority, a group the Confederate government did not wish to offend. The commander of Virginia's forces, Major General Robert E. Lee, sent cautions against precipitate action. "I am concerned at the feeling evinced in Maryland," Lee wrote Jackson on May 12, and

urged him "if possible to confine yourself to a strictly defensive course." To Jackson, the words "if possible" permitted him to exercise his discretion, which he proceeded to do forthwith.

To lay a groundwork for action, Jackson in mid-May registered an official complaint with the B & O Railroad, charging that his men found "their repose disturbed" by the trains passing through Harpers Ferry at night. B & O officials began limiting their freight runs through Jackson's domain to the daylight hours. Next, Jackson protested that the daytime traffic was interfering with his periods of drill and troop instruction, and he demanded that B & O trains traverse his lines only between 11 a.m. and 1 p.m. Reported John Imboden: "We then had, for two hours every day, the liveliest railroad in America."

Then Jackson moved. On May 23, when the tracks were crowded with heavily laden trains, his troops suddenly sealed off both ends of his 32-mile-long sector, capturing 56 locomotives and more than 300 cars.

Among the rich booty gathered in Jackson's operations against the B & O was an unexpected bonus. On a freight car bound for a Federal stable was a runty nag that for some reason struck Jackson's fancy. Intending it as a gift for Anna, he scrupulously counted out its purchase price to his quartermaster. But before he could present the little steed to his wife, Jackson grew so fond of it that he adopted it as his own. Perhaps only Robert E. Lee's magnificent gray, Traveller, was to become better known than Little Sorrel as a war horse in the Civil War.

Having stretched his mandate in the matter of the trains, Jackson reverted quickly to punctilio. As part of the Confederacy's assumption of military authority over state forces, Brigadier General Joseph E. Johnston, C.S.A., arrived at Harpers Ferry on May 24 to take command from Colonel Thomas J. Jackson, Virginia Volunteers. However, Jackson had received no official notification of the change, and Johnston had brought none with him. That being the case, Jackson courteously but firmly refused to turn over the reins "until I receive further instructions." The impasse was resolved only when Johnston rummaged about in his papers and finally found a document, signed in Lee's name by Lee's aide-de-camp, which referred to "General J. E. Johnston, commanding officer at Harpers Ferry."

Johnston, himself a stickler for correct military procedures, held no hard feelings.

Instead, he quickly appointed Jackson to command one of the three brigades he was forming for what would eventually be known as the Army of the Valley. Fearing that his force of about 6,500 would be outflanked by 18,000 Federals under General Robert Patterson who were threatening the line of the Potomac, Johnston in mid-June withdrew to Winchester, 30 miles southwest of Harpers Ferry. Jackson's 1st Brigade was dispatched to Martinsburg, 20 miles northwest of Harpers Ferry, with orders to feel out the enemy and to destroy all the B & O rolling stock it could lay its hands on. Near Martinsburg, Jackson would link up with Lieutenant Colonel J.E.B. Stuart, a young cavalry officer who was already establishing a reputation for being both dependable and dashing.

Jackson was delighted by the opportunity to do harm to the enemy — and, as always when he was given special responsibility, his physical ailments vanished. "I am bivouacking," he wrote Anna. "I sleep out of doors without any cover except my bedding, but have not felt any inconvenience from it in the way of impaired health." He would have felt even better if he had known he would soon draw blood.

Early on July 2, Patterson's men streamed across the Potomac north of Martinsburg, at Williamsport — under the watchful eye of J.E.B. Stuart. By 7:30 a.m., a hard-riding courier had brought the news from Stuart to Jackson, outside Martinsburg.

Jackson's orders from Johnston had been most explicit: He was to determine the enemy's strength. If Patterson was advancing in force, Jackson was to fall back as far as need be; under no circumstances was he to become involved in a general engagement.

Amid an assortment of camel-back engines and coal-carrying gondolas, railroad workers assemble in the Baltimore & Ohio yard at Martinsburg. The roundhouse and workshops, along with 42 locomotives and 305 railroad cars, were put to the torch by Jackson's 1st Brigade in June 1861.

Very well. Jackson determined upon a reconnaissance in force, and within minutes Colonel Kenton Harper's 5th Virginia Regiment (known within the brigade as the Fighting 5th for its brawling in camp) was on the march toward Falling Waters, site of a country church about five miles south of Williamsport. Jackson himself would accompany the expedition, and Colonel Harper would be supported by a battery of light artillery under Captain William N. Pendleton, a West Pointer who had turned clergyman and become the pastor of Lexington's Episcopal church.

Near Falling Waters, Federal skirmishers came probing forward along both sides of a highway and were taken under sharp and unexpected fire by Confederates partly concealed in woods. The skirmishers recoiled, and some brash young Confederates, who had taken cover in a house and a barn, started to give chase. But Jackson called them back.

By now the Federal skirmishers had reformed and, followed by two regiments of infantry, were coming on with a rush. The time had arrived for Jackson to obey orders and avoid a pitched battle. Keeping his men in line, he began a grudging retreat. The inexperienced Federals, concluding mistakenly that Jackson was defeated, sent a column down the highway in pursuit. At this point, a well-placed shot from one of Pendleton's guns sent the Federals flying back toward Falling Waters in disarray. Later, Jackson's men said gleefully that just before firing, the Reverend Dr. Pendleton had raised his eyes to heaven and pronounced a benediction on the enemy: "Lord, have mercy on their souls."

Meanwhile, Stuart and his cavalrymen

had split off from Jackson's main body to attempt a flank attack. Stuart, in the confusion, lost contact with his own troopers and, riding alone, sighted a sizable group of Federal infantrymen. Like many another Confederate in those early days of the War, Stuart was still wearing his old U.S. Army uniform. Thus disguised, he approached the Federal soldiers as if he were one of them— and then shouted suddenly: "Throw down your arms or you are all dead men!" The Federals not only obeyed but flung themselves flat on their faces. At that point, Stuart's men rode up and helped their commander collect 49 prisoners.

By the time the little action was done, Jackson was at Big Spring, two and a half miles south of Martinsburg, where Patterson had prudently halted.

In his first confrontation with the enemy, Jackson found cause for satisfaction: His troops had inflicted about an equal number of casualties as the two dozen men they had lost. Moreover, he had ably synchronized his infantry and artillery and had earned the admiration of his men by showing not the slightest trace of a flinch when a cannonball had smashed into a tree beside him.

"I am very thankful," he wrote Anna, "that an ever-kind Providence made me an instrument in carrying out General Johnston's orders so successfully." As for the Union's General Patterson, he reported that he had been opposed by a force of 3,500— almost 10 times Jackson's actual number at Falling Waters. It was the first of many occasions when Jackson's extreme vigor would persuade a Federal commander to overestimate greatly his numerical strength. The brush with Jackson would be more than enough to keep Patterson at a respectful dis-

tance, for he was an elderly, cautious officer.

A few days later, Jackson rejoined Johnston near Winchester, where he found awaiting him a commission as brigadier general in the Confederate Army.

On the morning of July 18, Johnston received alarming news via Richmond from General Pierre Gustave Toutant Beauregard. Near Manassas Junction, more than 60 miles southeast of Winchester, Beauregard's forces ranged along Bull Run were being threatened by a Federal army under Brigadier General Irvin McDowell.

Johnston immediately ordered his army to move out, though he gave no hint of the mission or destination. By about noon, the men were on the road, with General Jackson's 1st Brigade in the van. This was the first of the grueling marches for which Jackson and his troops would become famous.

The start was less than auspicious. The day was hot, the road was dusty and, since they were heading southeast, the men were disgruntled at the thought of turning their backs on Patterson. After an hour and a half of straggling and grumbling, Jackson's brigade was called to a halt to hear an officer relay a message from Johnston. The Federals had struck at Blackburn's Ford in a skirmish preliminary to the full-scale fighting at Bull Run. "The commanding general hopes that his troops will step out like men," the officer read, "and make a forced march to save the country."

The effect of the announcement was electric. "The soldiers rent the air with shouts of joy," Jackson wrote, "and all was eagerness and animation where before there had been only lagging and uninterested obedience."

Swinging out in new stride, the 1st Bri-

Jackson stands fast at the Battle of Bull Run in a drawing depicting the moment when he received his famous nickname. Afterward Jackson wrote his wife: "Whilst great credit is due to other parts of our gallant army, God made my brigade more instrumental than any other."

gade marched eleven miles to Millwood, where it briefly paused for food and rest. Later, in gathering dusk, the men stripped down and, with their clothes hoisted on musket barrels, waded across the waist-deep Shenandoah River. Then, in deep darkness, they moved four abreast up the steep slope of the Blue Ridge and through Ashby's Gap. Finally, at 2 a.m., they halted at the village of Paris on the eastern side of the mountains. In 14 hours, the raw troops had covered almost 20 steep and rugged miles. It was an exceptional performance.

Utterly exhausted, the troops collapsed in their tracks; making the rounds, Jackson found that even the sentries were slumbering. He let them sleep, and for the rest of the night the brigade's guard was mounted by one man, the commanding general.

At dawn, the men were again on the road, this time for a six-mile hike to the Manassas Gap Railroad depot at Piedmont. There they were loaded aboard hastily assembled freight cars and transported 34 miles to Manassas Junction.

Fought on July 21 beneath a cruel sun, the battle called Manassas by the Confederates and Bull Run by the Federals was a confused melee involving armies whose desperate courage was sad compensation for their inexperience. It was won for the Confederates by the presence of Johnston's troops from the Valley—and by the individual initiative of four brigade commanders, including Jackson, who had, without waiting for orders, left their assigned positions and marched to the sound of firing on Beauregard's left.

At a critical moment in the battle, when Confederate General Barnard Bee was attempting to stiffen his wavering troops, he was heard by some to shout, "There is Jackson, standing like a stone wall! Rally behind the Virginians!" That injunction, uttered shortly before Bee fell mortally wounded, conferred upon Jackson his unforgettable nickname. But to the Stonewall Brigade's rank and file, Jackson was otherwise known: They called him "Old Blue Light," a slang expression referring to his rigid piety, or simply "Old Jack."

In effect, the battle at Bull Run completed the military education that had begun on Jackson's first day at the United States Military Academy, and that he would soon take with him to the new Army of the Valley.

Like so many other Civil War commanders on both sides, Jackson's tactics early in the fighting were derived from the lessons he had been taught at West Point and from his field experiences during the Mexican War. Those lessons stressed that attacks be brought to victorious climax by a vigorous bayonet charge.

That tactic had served the United States infantry well against the Mexican Army, whose fire from smoothbore muskets was so slow and weak as to enable the Americans to come to close quarters and finish off the enemy with cold steel. "My orders was to make free use of the bayonet," said Jackson's ungrammatical military hero, General Zachary Taylor.

Steel appealed to Jackson, and he passionately believed in the bayonet. At Bull Run, when General Bee lamented that the Union seemed to be carrying the day, Jackson responded: "Sir, we'll give them the bayonet." And as the affray approached its end, Jackson exhorted his men to "fire and give them the bayonet; and when you charge, yell like furies!"

In fact, the day of the bayonet was ending. It was being rendered obsolete by the vastly increased range and killing power of rifled weapons, which as the war progressed cut down charging troops before they could use their steel. Moreover, even on those infrequent occasions when forces would grapple in hand-to-hand combat, there would be some instinct within the Civil War soldier to eschew the bayonet in favor of bashing his enemy's skull with a clubbed musket.

As a result, during a three-month period that included six major battles, Federal surgeons treated a scant 37 bayonet wounds. General John B. Gordon, a lawyer who became one of the South's hardest fighters, had nothing but scorn for the weapon. "The bristling points and the glitter of the bayonets were fearful to look upon as they were levelled in front of a charging line," Gordon wrote. "But they were rarely reddened with blood." Indeed, he continued, the bayonet's best use was "to impress the soldier's imagination, as the loud-sounding and ludicrous gongs are supposed to stiffen the backs and steady the nerves of the grotesque soldiers of China."

Jackson, however, like many other commanders, remained excessively devoted to the bayonet. But in abundant compensation, he brought to the battlefield great personal powers. His leadership was incandescent, his pugnacity was beyond measure, and his weak eyes were keen enough when it

Recruits for the Army of the Valley step to the cadences of fife and drum at Woodstock, Virginia, in the fall of 1861. Valley men adored Jackson for his deeds at Bull Run. When he was appointed to lead them, Secretary of War Judah P. Benjamin wrote him: "The people have made constant appeals that to you in whom they have confidence should their defense be assigned."

came to judging ground. His unyielding self-assurance, which had sometimes served him poorly, was a priceless asset in battle. He had, wrote General Gordon, who first saw Jackson at Bull Run, an "implicit faith in his own judgment when once made up. He would formulate that judgment, risk his last man on its correctness, and deliver the stunning blow, while others less gifted were hesitating and debating."

Moreover, he was able to take fullest advantage of the other tactics suggested by textbooks that had been in vogue at West Point. He entertained a wholesome respect for the flank attack as an alternative to the frontal charge; to Jackson, the enemy's flank was endlessly inviting. And he made a fetish of surprise as a tactical weapon. "Always mystify, mislead and surprise the enemy, if possible," he said. "The other rule is, never fight against heavy odds if by any possible maneuvering you can hurl your own force on only a part, and that the weakest part, of your enemy and crush it. Such tactics will win every time." As commander in the Valley, Jackson would have plenty of opportunity to mystify and mislead vastly superior forces.

After his stirring farewell to the 1st Virginia Brigade near Bull Run on November 4, Jackson set out for Winchester to take charge of Confederate forces in the Shenandoah. With two aides he rode about five miles to Manassas Junction, where they boarded a train heading west through the Manassas Gap in the Blue Ridge Mountains. After descending into the Shenandoah Valley, the train passed through the town of Front Royal, and 10 miles later skirted the northern end of Massanutten Mountain, which roughly parallels the Blue Ridge for 45 miles. At dusk Jackson and his aides finally reached the little town of Strasburg. Despite the late hour and the wearying train ride, Jackson refused to spend the night there. His party started north on horseback and covered the 18 miles to Winchester before midnight.

In all of the Shenandoah Valley, no place was to be fought for more fiercely and frequently than Winchester, the pleasant little colonial town that was, among other things, the hub for nine important roadways. Confederate control of Winchester offered the inviting possibilities of invasions into Maryland or Pennsylvania, or a movement against Washington; it also provided a base for raids against the B & O. Conversely, Federal occupation of Winchester would provide a staging area for incursions up the Valley, enhance the security of the Union's territory and promise greater protection for the B & O. As an astounding consequence, Winchester would change hands no fewer than 72 times during the War.

It was there, early on the morning of November 5, 1861, that General Jackson established his headquarters and notified Richmond that he had taken command.

A Cruel Winter's March

"If a man had told me 12 months ago that men could stand such hardships, I would have called him a fool."

LIEUTENANT JAMES H. LANGHORNE, STONEWALL BRIGADE, ON THE MARCH TO ROMNEY

2

In Winchester, General Jackson found a situation not at all to his liking. His Army of the Valley faced 18,000 Federals under Major General Nathaniel P. Banks holding western Maryland along the bank of the Potomac. In addition, more than 22,000 Federals led by Brigadier General William S. Rosecrans were established in western Virginia, just across the Alleghenies. And, of most immediate concern, Brigadier General Benjamin F. Kelley and his 5,000 Federals had recently captured the village of Romney, posing a threat to Jackson's western flank and even to his headquarters. General Kelley pointed out to his superiors that "from here to Winchester it is 40 miles, by the Northwestern turnpike, a very fine road. Should you desire to strike an offensive blow on Winchester, this is the position to concentrate."

To counter these forces, Jackson had pitiable resources. Scattered in little infantry and cavalry detachments were 1,651 militiamen armed with converted flintlocks and desperately short of ammunition; the largest group, numbering only 442, was stationed in Winchester. In addition, Jackson could call upon 485 undisciplined cavalry troopers under Colonel Angus McDonald, a 60-year-old Southern patriot whose rheumatic afflictions would soon force him to retire in favor of his flamboyant second-in-command, Lieutenant Colonel Turner Ashby. Finally, Jackson possessed two artillery pieces, which the gunners did not know how to load.

On his first day in command, Jackson did the little he could. He ordered his dispersed militiamen to concentrate at Winchester. He issued a call for all Valley militia not already in the field. And he dispatched his adjutant, Colonel J.T.L. Preston, to warn Richmond that at present the Shenandoah Valley was "defenseless." In fact, the weakness of the Valley defenses was so obvious that it had even been recognized by the Confederate Secretary of War, Judah P. Benjamin, whose ignorance of military matters was surpassed only by his chronic optimism. Even before Preston arrived, Benjamin had decided to send Jackson the Stonewall Brigade, which the general had so recently left.

Jackson had ambitious plans for his meager reinforcements. It was the measure of this obdurate fighting man that he meant to use them not to cover a retreat or even to conduct a static defense, but to attack the preponderant numbers arrayed against him.

His plans were unrealistic. During the next five months, Jackson would have to retreat often—not only from the enemy but also from positions he took in quarrels with colleagues. His worst military defeat, coming at the end of this period, would drive him from the field near a hamlet named Kernstown. Yet through all the vicissitudes, one thing was constant: Jackson nurtured his resolve to do terrible damage to the enemy.

A little more than two weeks after he took command, Jackson announced his aggressive intent in a letter to Secretary Benjamin.

Stonewall Jackson carried this U.S. Army sword with him throughout the Valley Campaign. Unlike more flamboyant generals who often raised their swords to rouse their troops on the battlefield, Jackson drew his so rarely that it eventually rusted in its scabbard.

The letter, dated November 20, revealed Jackson's strategic grasp and forecast his Valley Campaign. An offensive movement in the Valley, Jackson reasoned, might deceive Federal authorities into thinking he had been reinforced by General Joseph Johnston with troops from the Manassas-Centreville area. Believing that, even the unadventurous George McClellan, who had been named general in chief of the U.S. Army on November 1, might be tempted to attack Johnston's supposedly weakened army. Should McClellan move, Jackson pledged, the Valley army would turn from whatever it was doing and rush to Johnston's side. In short, the triumph at Bull Run might be repeated.

Jackson's plan did not end with McClellan's defeat. Thereafter, he argued, his troops could return to the Valley and then "move rapidly westward to the waters of the Monongahela and Little Kanawha" in Virginia's Allegheny region. "I deem it of very great importance that Northwestern Virginia be occupied by Confederate troops this winter," he continued.

Such were Jackson's long-range goals. His immediate object was to recapture Romney. That little mountain town dominated the fertile valley of the Potomac's South Branch. Through Romney passed the turnpike to Winchester, as well as a road that ran southwest through the Alleghenies to Monterey, intersecting there with the vital highway from Staunton to Parkersburg, on the Ohio River. Arcing around Romney at an average

distance of 20 miles was a 60-mile stretch of the Baltimore & Ohio tracks, previously put out of commission by Confederate raids but now being repaired by Federal work crews. Retaking Romney — as Jackson wrote to General Johnston — would drive a wedge between the Federals in the Alleghenies and Banks's contingent, preventing them from joining forces around Martinsburg.

To set his scheme in motion, Jackson would need help, and he knew just what he wanted. The Confederate Army of the Northwest, now commanded by Brigadier General William W. Loring after a dismal mountain campaign under Robert E. Lee, was doing little more in the Alleghenies than guarding the Staunton-Parkersburg road. Jackson wrote Benjamin of his plan and said, "Through the blessing of God, who has thus far so wonderfully prospered our cause, much more may be expected from General Loring's troops than can be expected from them where they are."

Both Benjamin and Johnston endorsed the operation against Romney, though the general thought that Jackson's overall plan "proposes more than can well be accomplished." Benjamin cautiously set about trying to arrange the transfer of Loring's troops to the Valley for the move on Romney.

Benjamin's discretion was well-advised, for Loring was a touchy man who demanded careful treatment. He had been soldiering for a very long while, first as a boy in Florida's Seminole War of the 1830s; then as an

45

officer in Mexico, where he lost an arm at Chapultepec; later in New Mexico chasing Indians. Clearly he had been jealous when Lee had been named over him to command the Army of the Northwest, and he had evidently taken out his displeasure by conducting all his operations as slowly as possible.

In broaching the plan to Loring, Benjamin merely expressed the hope that the Army of the Northwest would join Jackson. Loring meditated for a while, then consented — on his own terms. He would require two, possibly three weeks of "every exertion" to get ready to march. Moreover, he would bring with him only three of his four brigades — about 6,000 men — leaving behind the command of Brigadier General Edward Johnson to guard the Allegheny passes.

Jackson had little choice but to wait for Loring before commencing his move against Romney. Meanwhile, he fretfully sought other occupations for his Valley army, which was chafing at the boredom and artificial disciplines of camp life.

A special problem was posed by the Stonewall Brigade, whose mood had changed radically since the troops had learned in early November that they were going to rejoin Jackson. "Then there was joy in the camp," Private John O. Casler had written; the Valley men were happy to be returning to their beloved Shenandoah, and they looked forward to enjoying the hospitality of Winchester. They were swiftly disillusioned.

Arriving at Winchester on November 12, they were marched straight through town and sent into camp four and a half miles to the north. Furloughs were forbidden, Winchester was placed off limits, and Jackson set up a cordon of militiamen to enforce his edicts. Even officers were denied entry into Winchester unless they could show passes from Jackson's headquarters.

The weather made things even worse for the men. An unusually bitter winter set in. Wild winds shrieked down from the mountains, and the men often had to brace the tent poles to keep their flimsy cotton tents from being swept away. Cold rain and sleet pelted the brigade for days on end. Influenza and measles were soon epidemic.

Jackson countered the spreading illness and grumbling in characteristic fashion. His wife, Anna, noted, "He remembered the saying of Napoleon, that 'an active winter's campaign is less liable to produce disease than a sedentary life by camp-fires in winter quarters.' " The march against Romney was Jackson's main remedy. But until Loring's creeping columns arrived, he decided to occupy his men with a lesser objective that lay close at hand.

Extending 185 miles alongside the Potomac from Cumberland, Maryland, to Washington was the 60-foot-wide Chesapeake & Ohio Canal, capable of handling barges with loads weighing up to 100 tons. With the B & O tracks broken, the Federals depended heavily on the canal to provide their stoves with Appalachian coal. Jackson decided to cut this artery near Martinsburg at Dam No. 5, one of a series of dams that regulated the depth of the canal waters.

He set out before dawn on December 16 with the Stonewall Brigade, a militia brigade and the Rockbridge Artillery, a remarkable battery whose original muster included 35 college graduates (seven with master's degrees) and 25 theology students. By dusk the next day, Jackson's forces were peering over the bluffs of the Potomac at the site of their

This portrait of Stonewall Jackson, with a romantic view of the Shenandoah Valley behind him, was painted from a photograph taken at Winchester in 1862. When the photographer noticed that a jacket button was missing, Jackson produced the button from his pocket, asked for a needle and thread, and sewed it back on himself.

Defending Dam No. 5 on the Potomac River near Williamsport, Maryland, a company of the 13th Massachusetts Volunteers exchanges fire with Stonewall Jackson's troops on the opposite shore in December 1861.

target. Thirty Irish volunteers of the 27th Virginia descended to the dam and put up a camouflaging brush screen around the area. Their work done before dawn, the Irishmen rejoined their comrades, who had shivered the night away — Jackson had banned campfires to keep their position concealed.

Despite such precautions, the enemy that day spotted his force and began a lively bombardment from the Maryland side of the river. Private George Neese, a Confederate gunner under enemy shelling for the first time, later said, "I laid so close to the ground that it seemed to me I flattened out a little."

For the next few days, Jackson and his men holed up during the daylight hours and worked by night; waist-deep in the frigid waters, they labored with crowbars, picks and axes to tear a hole in the dam.

Several times the men came under renewed fire from the Maryland shore. As a decoy Jackson sent his militia brigade upriver with orders to attract as much attention as possible. The Federals followed, and Jackson's wrecking crew, now free to work, finally succeeded in breaching the dam.

On the way back to Winchester, Jackson may have smiled with satisfaction at the results of his sally. He rarely laughed, and when he did it was a soundless grimace that made it obvious, as an aide wrote, that "he had never laughed enough to learn how." In any case, the last laugh belonged to the Federals. For all of the Confederates' enterprise and travail, the damage they did to the dam was repaired within two days.

When Jackson returned to Winchester on December 23, he found that only one of Loring's brigades, under the command of Colonel William B. Taliaferro, had yet arrived in

town. The others were still dawdling along the way. Indeed, one brigade stopped near Strasburg on Christmas Day and imbibed so much eggnog that when the men were ordered to resume their march, some of them collapsed on the road. Not until December 26 were all of Loring's men at Winchester, bringing the total of Jackson's force to 7,500 volunteers, 2,200 militia and 650 cavalry.

On December 29, the persistent cold relented, and on New Year's Eve, Jackson issued his marching orders. To aid in identification during the confusion of battle, all men were required to carry three-inch-wide white bands to wear around their hats. At 6 o'clock the next morning they would step out toward an undisclosed destination.

And so, on New Year's Day, 1862, Jackson's tiny army sallied forth. As one man recalled, the day was "springlike in its mildness," and the troops behaved as if they were on a lark. They worked up a bit of a sweat and many of them got rid of their burdensome overcoats and blankets, either depositing them in company wagons or simply strewing them along the road.

Then, suddenly, the fair weather turned foul. A chilling wind whistled out of the northwest, the temperature plunged, snow and sleet fell, and the shivering men began wishing for the gear they had so blithely discarded. But the supply wagons had fallen far behind the marching columns. For hundreds of men there would be no greatcoats or blankets that night.

To Jackson, the best route between two points was rarely a straight line. Instead of taking the fine turnpike that went directly to Romney, he had headed northwest on a wagon-rutted road that led to the mineral-water resort of Bath, 35 miles northeast of

Confederate Brigadier General William Loring, who lost an arm in the Mexican War, condemned what he called Stonewall Jackson's "utter disregard for human suffering" during the winter campaign near Bath. Loring charged that "a portion of my command was rendered unfit for active duty by marches of cruel severity."

Romney and about 40 miles from Winchester. The weather continued to worsen, and the struggling army made only eight miles that day before stopping at Pughtown. That night the men shared what blankets they had left and slept huddled together in what a private called "hog fashion."

The next morning, the men set out into a thickening blizzard. Toward the end of the day's wretched march, some of Loring's regiments became hopelessly intermixed while trying to cross an icy bog. Worse yet, the supply wagons fell even farther behind — and since most of the men, in the rash manner of young troops, had long since consumed their marching rations, hunger pangs were now added to their miseries.

William Taliaferro (*seated, left*), promoted to brigadier general after the Romney march, is photographed with fellow officers and a saluting orderly of the Virginia Militia. Jackson disliked Taliaferro and protested his appointment to the Valley army with a stinging complaint: "Through God's blessing my command, though small, is efficient, and I respectfully request its efficiency may not be injured by assigning to it inefficient officers."

For the second successive day, the army covered barely eight miles, halting for the night at a place called Unger's Store. That night, recalled a soldier who did sentry duty, "the soles of the shoes actually froze to the ground."

On the morning of January 3, Jackson deliberately bypassed a crossroad at Unger's Store that led west through Bloomery Gap to Romney. Instead, he kept the troops marching on toward Bath. The town was held by about 1,400 Federals who could attack the right flank of any Confederate move against Romney from the east. Jackson meant to end that threat. At the very least he would drive the Federal garrison back across the Potomac. At best he hoped to trap and capture the enemy force, then cross the river to destroy Federal supply depots at Hancock, Maryland, and to cut the telegraph lines between Romney and western Maryland.

The day's march was an ordeal. Colonel Taliaferro began by deliberately heading his brigade in the wrong direction—back to the wagons carrying food. The troops slipped and slithered across the frozen bog that had given them so much trouble the day before; after eating, they were still so weary that they required two hours of rest before retracing their steps.

During one of the many delays that day, the ill-tempered General Loring exploded. He was so infuriated by an order from Jackson to keep his men moving that he announced to all around him, "By God, Sir, this is the damnedest outrage ever perpetrated in the annals of history, keeping my men out here in the cold without food."

The same day Jackson had an unpleasant encounter with his successor as commander of the Stonewall Brigade, Brigadier General Richard B. Garnett. To almost everyone but Jackson, Garnett seemed just what a soldier ought to be. Scion of an aristocratic family from the Virginia Tidewater, he was a West Pointer whose cousin Robert Garnett had been the first Confederate general to be killed during the War. One of the Army's boldest Indian fighters, Richard Garnett was a comely man with dark wavy hair and a neatly trimmed beard. And he looked after his men well—so well that Jackson thought he coddled them.

Now Jackson's suspicions seemed confirmed. About 10 miles short of Bath, when the Stonewall Brigade's wagons at long last caught up with the column, Garnett ordered a halt to feed the famished men, some of whom had not eaten in 30 hours. At that point Jackson rode up and asked angrily why the brigade had stopped.

"I have halted to let the men cook their rations," Garnett explained.

"There is no time for that," Jackson snapped.

"But it is impossible for the men to march further without them," said Garnett.

"I never found anything impossible with this brigade!" Jackson said, then rode away. But it boded ill for the Valley army that he never forgave Garnett.

At dusk, Jackson finally arrived outside Bath. There he learned from local inhabitants that a road ran westward from the town across a massive ridge named Warm Spring Mountain. To cut off enemy troops who might try to escape in that direction—which would take them toward Romney—Jackson sent his militia around the southern flank of the mountain. Then he ordered one of Loring's brigades, under Colonel William Gilham, to drive straight into Bath.

Jackson's troops plod through the snow during their advance on Romney in this sketch by a soldier who made the bitterly cold march. An officer wrote, "Two battles would not have done as much injury as hard weather and exposure have effected."

The march around Warm Spring Mountain was a difficult maneuver — well beyond the awkward capacities of the militiamen. They were stopped cold by a few trees the enemy had felled across their path.

The brigade under Colonel Gilham did not do much better. Gilham was quite literally a textbook commander. He had been Professor of Infantry Tactics at VMI while Jackson was there and had written a *Manual of Instruction for the Volunteers and Militia of the United States* (after Fort Sumter "Confederate States" was substituted for "United States" in the title). Now that an opportunity had arisen to put his education to practice, he moved timidly toward town, brushed up against Federal skirmishers and recoiled as if bitten. When Jackson sent instructions for Gilham to charge as if he meant it, Loring countermanded the order. Thus a bad day ended on a dismal note.

Next day the militia tried again on the west side of Warm Spring Mountain, but the waiting Federals took them by surprise and sent them scampering. Gilham, moving again toward Bath, stopped a half mile from town when he saw enemy troops on the mountain. With the morning and early afternoon wasted, Jackson disgustedly sent his cavalry galloping into Bath under one of his staff officers; the general himself followed close after the horsemen and, as he wrote in his scathing report of the action, "entered the town in advance of the skirmishers" under Gilham. The Federal infantry was gone, having peaceably departed, some across the mountain to the west and others northward across the Potomac to Hancock.

By the time Jackson had reached the Potomac in pursuit, darkness was falling and he could do no more than fire a few shells at

Confederate Brigadier General Richard B. Garnett, shown here in a prewar photograph, remained a great admirer of Stonewall Jackson even after Jackson had him arrested for retreating at Kernstown. "Had he conferred with me on that occasion," Garnett claimed, "I am confident all cause of complaint would have been avoided."

Hancock from the two guns he had managed to bring up. Next morning he sent an emissary across the river and into Hancock under a flag of truce to demand that the town be surrendered within an hour. When the Federal commander declined, Jackson briefly bombarded the village, then ordered a bridge constructed across the Potomac two miles above Hancock.

On January 6, however, Jackson changed his mind, reporting that the Hancock garrison was reinforced "to such an extent as to induce me to believe that my object could not be accomplished without a sacrifice of life, which I felt unwilling to make." Next morning he set his men in motion back toward Unger's Store and the crossroad to Romney.

The march was one that the troops would remember to the end of their days. As they moved over a treacherous sheet of ice covered by six inches of snow, the temperature dropped — and kept dropping until it reached about 20 degrees below zero. Lurching ahead on numbed and frostbitten feet, the men slipped and fell time and again; one of them remembered the sound of his comrades "hitting the road with a thud like that of a pile driver."

Horses were in even greater distress, for Jackson, with a failure of foresight unusual for him, had neglected to order the animals roughshod for winter. Private Casler saw "one horse in each team down nearly all the time. As soon as one would get up, another would be down, and sometimes all four at once." An artilleryman later recalled that "from one horse's knees there were icicles of blood which reached nearly to the ground."

Jackson was everywhere. On at least one occasion he put his shoulder to the wheel of a wagon to help prevent it from sliding backward down an icy slope. But he showed little sympathy for his army in its ordeal. As one of his staff officers wrote, Jackson "classed all who were weak and weary, who fainted by the wayside, as men wanting in patriotism. If a man's face was as white as cotton and his pulse so low you could scarcely feel it, he looked upon him merely as an inefficient soldier and rode off impatiently."

By the time the army struggled into Unger's Store on January 8 it was in woeful condition. One of Loring's brigades reported 500 men sick; another reported 300 sick. With his ranks depleted and with snow and sleet continuing, Jackson had no option but to wait at Unger's Store while the men rested and farriers reshod the horses with ice calks. There he stayed for four days. Finally, on January 13, his cavalry reported that the enemy, against all expectations and having grossly overestimated Jackson's strength, had abandoned Romney.

The trek from Unger's Store to Romney, undertaken in driving sleet, was yet another ordeal. An infantryman recalled that when the Stonewall Brigade arrived late on January 14, "every soldier's clothing was a solid cake of ice," and there were "icicles two inches long hanging from the hair and whiskers of every man."

Loring's brigades took two days longer; one regiment managed to move only 500 yards in a day. Unaccustomed to Jackson's ways and enraged by the suffering to which he had subjected them, Loring's men jeered and hissed when he rode among them. He would soon give the troops further cause for disgruntlement.

Jackson reported with some satisfaction that the entire expedition had cost him only four men killed and 28 wounded. He now prepared to take up winter quarters. One militia brigade would be stationed at Bath to guard against a Federal crossing from Hancock. Another would be posted at Martinsburg on the lookout for an enemy incursion from that direction. Loring's brigades would remain at Romney to ensure the security of the South Branch Valley. And the Stonewall Brigade would return with Jackson to Winchester, where it would be within supporting range of all the outposts.

The plan did not sit well with Loring's men. Despite the beauty of the surrounding countryside, Romney was a cheerless place. Garbage was strewn through the dirt streets, and a powerful stench rose from the courthouse, where the departing enemy had left tons of rotting meat. On January 25, two days after Jackson had ridden hurriedly back to Winchester, 11 of Loring's brigade and regimental commanders signed an unsoldierly petition to Loring. It said: "Instead of finding, as expected, a little repose during midwinter, we are ordered to remain at this place. Our position at and near Romney is one of the most disagreeable and unfavorable that could well be imagined."

One of the officers who signed the petition, Colonel Samuel Fulkerson of the 37th

Headgear for the Armies

Civil War soldiers wore an astonishing variety of headgear. Although both sides had dress regulations, the choice of a hat or cap was more often than not a matter of personal or regimental preference.

There were four basic styles of headgear: the broad-brimmed black felt 1858 U.S. Army hat, ornamented with a black ostrich feather; forage caps patterned af-ter the short-visored French kepis; assorted fezzes worn by Zouave outfits; and sundry civilian slouch hats.

Recruits on both sides liked headgear that made them look like soldiers, but comfort and practicality were their first considerations. The U.S. Army hat (*bottom row, second from right*) failed on both counts. "My new hat looks like the pic-

C.S. ENLISTED MAN'S KEPI

C.S. ARTILLERY OFFICER'S KEPI

C.S. OFFICER'S FORAGE CAP

C.S. SLOUCH HAT

tures you see of the Pilgrim fathers," one man wrote. "Hot, heavy, stiff and ill-looking," claimed another. Indeed, so unpopular were the hats that many units refused to accept them, or discarded them at the first opportunity.

More popular with Federal troops was the 1858 forage cap, with its high crown (*bottom row, far right*). "There is room for a wet sponge, green leaves, a handkerchief or other protection against the sun," a soldier declared. Still others preferred the jaunty, low-crowned kepi (*top row, second from right*), popularized by General McClellan.

Confederate regulations called for kepis, with a man's branch of service to be indicated by the color of the crown, and an officer's rank by gold braid. Most Confederate kepis, however, were plain gray because of dye and cloth shortages. Many men chose slouch hats in any case. "A man who has never been a soldier does not know the amount of comfort there is in a good soft hat," a Virginian said, "and how utterly useless is a 'soldier's hat' as they are generally made."

U.S. OFFICER'S MCCLELLAN-STYLE KEPI

U.S. ZOUAVE FEZ

U.S. OFFICER'S 1858 ARMY HAT

U.S. ENLISTED MAN'S FORAGE CAP

Virginia, also wrote a note of complaint to a political friend in Richmond. "This place is of no importance in a strategical point of view," he declared. "We have not been in as uncomfortable a place since we entered the service." Fulkerson showed his letter to Colonel Taliaferro, who added a poisonous postscript: "The best army I ever saw has been destroyed by bad marches and bad management. It is ridiculous. It will be suicidal to keep this command here."

When Loring received the petition, he wrote a covering note saying that it set forth "the true condition of this army" and sent it through channels to Jackson. Jackson dispatched it to the War Department with a brusque notation: "Respectfully forwarded, but disapproved."

To ensure that his officers' petition did not get stopped on its way to Richmond, Loring broke with protocol and went over his superior's head. He gave Colonel Taliaferro, who was about to depart for Richmond on leave, a copy of the petition and asked him to hand it personally to Jefferson Davis. Taliaferro did so, showing the President on a map the location of Loring's force.

Davis, Taliaferro wrote later, "did not hesitate to say at once that Jackson had made a mistake, and he ordered the concentration of the troops at Winchester by telegraph that same morning."

A decree changing Jackson's dispositions was sent through and signed by War Secretary Benjamin. Alleging that a Federal force was moving to cut off General Loring's command, the document stated flatly: "Order him back to Winchester immediately."

Upon receipt of the order, Jackson dutifully recalled Loring's command to Winchester. Then his indignation took over.

Thomas J. Jackson, a true Confederate hero, asked to be relieved of active duty.

"With such interference," he wrote Benjamin, "I cannot expect to be of much service in the field, and accordingly respectfully request to be ordered to report for duty to the superintendent of the Virginia Military Institute at Lexington. Should this application not be granted, I respectfully request that the President will accept my resignation from the Army."

The letter was dispatched to Jackson's immediate superior for forwarding to Richmond. General Johnston held onto it for several days in hopes of saving Jackson's career. He wrote Jackson, addressing him as "My Dear Friend" and saying, "Let me beg you to reconsider this matter." Pointing out that he too had been bypassed by Benjamin's order to Jackson, Johnston asked: "Is not that as great an official wrong to me as the order itself is to you? Let us dispassionately reason with the government on this subject of command."

When Johnston received no reply to his overture to the angry general, he decided he had no choice but to send Jackson's request on to Richmond. "Respectfully forwarded, with great regret," he wrote. "I don't know how the loss of this officer can be supplied."

Meanwhile, Jackson had been playing politics. On the same day he dispatched his official request to Benjamin through Johnston, he had sent an unofficial explanation to a friend and neighbor from his Lexington days — Virginia Governor John Letcher. "A single order like that of the Secretary's may destroy the entire fruits of a campaign," he wrote. "If I ever acquired, through the blessing of Providence, any influence over troops, this undoing of my work by the Secretary may greatly diminish that influence."

Letcher at once went to Benjamin's office. He found the Secretary distinctly uncomfortable at the stir he had caused and willing to discuss the Jackson matter. Exactly what terms were proposed for a reconciliation with Jackson remain unknown, but it is certain that Letcher was authorized to communicate them to Jackson. Letcher chose as his emissary another old friend of Jackson's, Congressman Alexander R. Boteler.

The details of Boteler's meeting with Jackson were never described by either man. But it is known that Boteler appealed strongly to Jackson's Confederate patriotism; it is possible that he relayed some sort of a promise from Benjamin not to interfere again in Jackson's legitimate exercise of command. At any event, Jackson finally acquiesced, writing to Governor Letcher and authorizing him to withdraw the resignation.

The dispute was not quite over, however. On the day after he agreed to remain at his post, Jackson formally charged Loring with neglect of duty and with conduct "subversive of good order and military discipline." But Davis and Benjamin did not permit Loring to be brought before a court-martial board; instead, they promoted him to major general and transferred him to Georgia.

With Loring out of the way, Jackson settled down to what his wife, who had come to stay with him in Winchester, called "as happy a winter as ever falls to the lot of mortals on this earth." That blissful state was soon brought to an end by the U.S. Army in the person of General Nathaniel P. Banks.

Back in July of 1861, shortly after the Union's General Robert Patterson had fallen into disgrace for allowing Joseph Johnston's army to escape the Valley and fight at Bull Run, a newspaper with some interesting information arrived at Patterson's headquarters on the Potomac. President Lincoln, it reported, had just made a major general out of Mr. N. P. Banks, a prominent Massachusetts politician.

The commander of the 2nd Massachusetts Regiment, Colonel George H. Gordon, who had known Banks slightly, was asked by other officers what he thought of the appointment. Gordon said that he doubted the report because Banks "has too much sense and good judgment to assume the responsibilities of such rank until he has fitted himself in subordinate situations to know something of a soldier's profession — in which . . ." Gordon, by his account, was about to add the words "he is now totally inexperienced," when there came a knock on the door. It was a courier with the announcement that Major General Banks would, within minutes, arrive to assume command from Patterson.

Colonel Gordon knew his man. Not only was Banks utterly innocent about arms and armies, but only a few years before he had bragged of that fact, saying that he was "not acquainted with the details of military matters, and personally have no pride in them."

Born in Waltham, Massachusetts, Banks as a boy had worked replacing empty bobbins in a cotton-textile factory for two dollars a week. After his subsequent rise to high place, Banks's humble background provided a title for a book by the Reverend William Makepeace Thayer: *The Bobbin Boy, or How Nat Got His Learning.*

Drawn into politics by his early and ardent interest in the temperance movement, Banks served for 10 terms in the U.S. House of Representatives. He was elected Speaker of the House after the longest contest in history (133 ballots taken over a nine-week period) and later became governor of Massachusetts. His affiliations were as shifting as his achievements were solid: He had been in turn a Democrat, a Know-Nothing (as the nativist members of the American Party were called) and a Republican; after the War he would turn again to the Democrats and then back to the Republicans.

No matter. Banks was undeniably a patriot, and Abraham Lincoln needed his support — even if it meant trying to make a soldier of him. Upon his appointment Banks became the fourth-ranking officer of the Federal Army, junior to only Winfield Scott, John C. Frémont and George McClellan. Banks was modest about his high rank. "Detail me where you will," he was quoted as saying. "It is my duty to obey."

He loved the soldier's life, especially the part that permitted him to review parades. "General Banks comes up with a multitudinous staff," said a Federal soldier of one such occasion. "The general removes his cap. He is splendid, his staff behind him is splendid. All is splendid." As even a Confederate prisoner later admitted, he was a "faultless-looking soldier" with his bright yellow gloves, gleaming boots, glittering spurs and horses picked more for their looks than their stamina. Only a recent growth of mustache refused to cooperate with his martial mien — it hung limply around his mouth.

Rarely have appearances been more deceiving. As a general, the Bobbin Boy of Massachusetts turned out to be a poor administrator and a feeble disciplinarian; one of his regiments got so unruly that it had to be disbanded. He disregarded maps and disdained to make personal reconnaissances.

Overall, said one of his subordinates, Brigadier General William B. Franklin, "an operation dependent on plenty of troops, rather than skill in handling them, was the only one which could have probability of success in his hands." In fact, Banks was amassing plenty of troops. By the end of February 1862, he would have at least 38,000 in Maryland, with the prospect of receiving others from northwestern Virginia when and if he crossed the Potomac. That he had not done so was hardly his fault. His army was caught in the middle of a tug of war between the Lincoln administration and its top commander, General George McClellan.

Both Lincoln and McClellan were determined to take Richmond, but that was the extent of their agreement. Abraham Lincoln favored the most direct approach to the Confederate capital: southwest to Manassas Junction, then due south through Fredericksburg. That route would have the advantage of keeping McClellan's force interposed between Johnston's retreating Confederates and Washington.

McClellan, however, had sired a grand plan for a flanking movement that might avoid a confrontation with Johnston's forces. What he had in mind was a giant amphibious operation. He would sail his army down Chesapeake Bay to Fort Monroe, whence it could march the 70 miles west up the Peninsula, the finger of land between the James and York Rivers, until finally it stood before Richmond.

Lincoln reluctantly agreed. But he was still worried about Washington, and he extracted from McClellan a pledge to leave behind a force sufficient to protect the capital and its environs. The number of troops constituting a sufficiency was for the moment left open, but it would soon become a subject of high controversy.

At about that point, Secretary of War Edwin M. Stanton imposed his own ideas on McClellan, insisting that the general secure the B & O tracks in the lower, or northern, Shenandoah Valley before making his massive move to the Peninsula. That was perfectly all right by McClellan. He had in any event planned to shift Banks eastward as part of the covering force for Washington while his own Army of the Potomac sailed south. It would require only an inconsiderable delay for Banks to pass over the Potomac, seize Winchester and thus safeguard the railroad before moving most of his force to Manassas Junction. In fact, said McClellan, he would join Banks to supervise the operation in person.

Banks himself was chafing to go. "The roads to Winchester are turnpikes and in tolerable condition," he reported on February 23, 1862. "The enemy is weak, demoralized and depressed." But then he added a note of caution: "We will not ask odds of fortune. Our force alone is not sufficient, but we will gladly risk it."

He soon had his chance. On the night of February 27, Stanton went to the White House and read to Lincoln a message saying that Banks had thrown a pontoon bridge across the Potomac at Harpers Ferry and had already pushed some men into Virginia.

That was encouraging. But before reading a second message, Stanton closed and locked the door to Lincoln's office, explaining: "The next is not so good." McClellan had arranged to move Banks's artillery and other equipment too weighty for the pontoons across the river on a bridge made of canalboats, which were supposed to have arrived

Brigadier General Alpheus S. Williams (*on horseback, far right*), a division commander in Banks's army, prepares to review his headquarters guard at Darnestown,

Maryland. The Federal camp, part of the ring of defenses around Washington, became a staging area for Banks's expedition to the Shenandoah Valley.

at Harpers Ferry by way of the Chesapeake & Ohio Canal. But the waterway's locks had proved too narrow for the canalboats. The heavy matériel remained on the Maryland side of the Potomac, and until it could be transported, McClellan would have to suspend the move against Winchester.

The next day, in an exchange of messages with Washington, McClellan proposed that, while supplying his troops in Virginia with the matériel they needed for an advance in force, he would occupy Charles Town and Bunker Hill, 40 miles northeast and 12 miles north of Winchester respectively. The capture of these towns would cover the rebuilding of the B & O track torn up beyond Harpers Ferry by the Confederates. Banks had little trouble capturing Charles Town and Bunker Hill. But McClellan informed Washington that he could not move against Jackson at Winchester "for many days." However, he assured his superiors, "you will be satisfied when I see you that I have acted wisely and have everything in hand."

Lincoln and Stanton were far from satisfied, but they could do little about it. McClellan ordered Banks to remain safely settled at Charles Town and at Bunker Hill.

McClellan's inertia was finally broken by the Confederates. General Joseph Johnston, deciding that his forward positions were at serious risk, began withdrawing south from the Manassas-Centreville area on March 7. Learning of the Confederate withdrawal on March 9, McClellan immediately ordered his armies to push forward on all fronts — including the Shenandoah Valley.

Given the go-ahead, Banks moved slowly, apparently much impressed by what appeared from a distance to be formidable Confederate fortifications on the hills north

of Winchester. Finally, on the morning of March 12, Banks's troops entered Winchester, only to find that Jackson's infantry had departed late the previous day. When other Federal officers expressed disappointment that Jackson had been permitted to get away without a fight, Colonel George Gordon predicted that "this chieftain would be apt, before the war closed, to give us an entertainment up to the utmost of our aspirations."

En route to the Shenandoah Valley, Federal troops under General Nathaniel Banks cross the Potomac River at Harpers Ferry on a pontoon bridge in February 1862. On the left are the pillars of the railroad bridge destroyed by the retreating Confederates in June 1861.

was a pipe dream and did not trouble to reply. Thus the orders he had issued Jackson on March 1 still held: The Valley army, remaining west of the Blue Ridge, was to move southward parallel to Johnston's withdrawal on the other side of the mountains. As he pulled back, Jackson should attempt to secure the Blue Ridge passes so as to prevent Banks from crossing the mountains and falling on Johnston's flank. What was more, Jackson was expected to be flexible enough to keep Banks occupied, preventing him from leaving the Valley by any route to reinforce McClellan.

Jackson had every intention of keeping Banks busy. On the 11th of March, as his Confederates were streaming out of Winchester, Jackson had anticipated that Banks would rush through the town in hot pursuit, and he planned to turn and strike the Federals in a rare night attack. But in a conference that evening with his commanders, he discovered that his troops had been allowed to march too far away from Winchester to make the attack. Still blazing with wrath as he rode out of Winchester, Jackson turned to an aide and said savagely: "That is the last council of war I will ever hold." He kept his word.

While Jackson withdrew at a leisurely rate to Mount Jackson, about 42 miles up the Valley, the Federals crept only 18 miles past Winchester to Strasburg; there Banks stationed 9,000 men under Brigadier General James Shields. A native of Ireland's County Tyrone, Shields was, like Banks, a highly successful politician, having served as a U.S. Senator from both Illinois and Minnesota. Unlike Banks, however, he was combative in fact as well as in words. Besides fighting in the Mexican War, he had once won a certain distinction by challenging Abraham Lincoln

Indeed, Jackson wanted to fight right away. Never mind that his current forces — 3,600 infantry, 600 cavalry and six batteries with 27 guns — were outnumbered more than 8 to 1 by Banks. On March 8 he had asked Johnston for some reinforcements, and in return offered him the cheery prospect that "a kind Providence may enable us to inflict a terrible wound."

Johnston apparently reckoned that this

to a duel over a seemingly slanderous political article. The duel never came off.

McClellan's moves to shift Banks across the Blue Ridge to Manassas Junction had already begun. One of Banks's divisions, under Brigadier General John Sedgwick, had marched east on March 14; another, under Brigadier General Alpheus Williams, departed a week later. Only Shields's division was to stay in the Valley, and on March 20 it started pulling back from Strasburg to Winchester, where it could best protect the B & O tracks. Banks himself would leave for a visit to Washington on March 23.

The various Federal movements were scouted out by Confederate cavalry under Turner Ashby, who sent a courier galloping to inform Jackson late on March 21. To Jackson, it was instantly clear that Banks was in the process of doing precisely what he himself had been ordered to prevent. The Valley army, moving fast, was on the road at dawn the next day.

While Jackson was hurrying north, Ashby was fighting. Prowling with 280 troopers on the afternoon of the 22nd, he clashed with Shields's pickets just south of Winchester in a brisk skirmish that ended only at sunset. The encounter had significant consequences. Shields, who had hurried to the scene, was wounded and carried into town; his command went to Colonel Nathan Kimball, a tough old veteran of the Mexican War who was a physician in peacetime.

Through his pain, Shields kept his wits about him. He directed that one part of his division be moved south of Winchester during the night. Another brigade marched north, as if it were abandoning Winchester, but soon halted and remained ready to move to the scene as soon as it received word

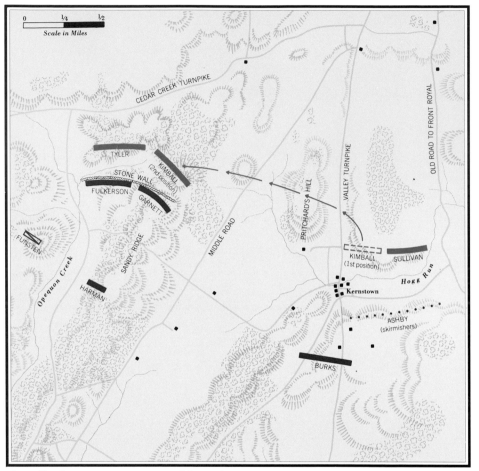

that Jackson was approaching the town.

That same night, Confederate loyalists from Winchester mistakenly told Ashby that Shields had left behind a rear guard of only four regiments, and that even these units were under orders to depart for Harpers Ferry on the morrow. At about 2 p.m. on the chill, windy afternoon of March 23, Jackson rode up to the tiny village of Kernstown, four miles south of Winchester, and Ashby greeted him with the happy news of the enemy's weakness.

Jackson now faced a dilemma. His men were weary, having already left 1,500 stragglers along the trail as they marched 25 miles on the 22nd and 16 more on this day. Even

At Kernstown on March 23, Jackson's brigades under Fulkerson and Garnett advanced against Erastus B. Tyler's Federal brigade on Sandy Ridge in an attempt to flank the right of the Federal line. Colonel Nathan Kimball countered the threat by shifting several regiments from the left to reinforce Tyler. Outnumbered, the Confederates were finally forced to withdraw.

more distressing, it was Sunday — a day Jackson took so seriously that he would not even post a letter if he thought it might be in transit on the Sabbath.

On the other hand, he had been looking all along for an opportunity to pounce upon an isolated fragment of Banks's host — and he would never have a better chance than this. Quickly, he overcame his doubts, explaining later to Anna, "I hope and pray to our Heavenly Father that I may never again be circumstanced as on that day. I believed that so far as our troops were concerned, necessity and mercy both called for the battle. Arms is a profession that, if its principles are adhered to for success, requires an officer to do what he fears may be wrong."

Without making a further reconnaissance, Jackson decided on his deployment. To his right front, east of the Valley Turnpike, the enemy appeared to be concentrated in an open wheat field; they were supported by two Federal batteries placed on a knoll, west of the highway, called Pritchard's Hill. An assault on the right would be hard going. So on that side nothing more than a holding action would be attempted; the assignment fell to Ashby's cavalrymen, supported by a small brigade under Colonel Jesse Burks.

The left looked better — much better. There, perhaps two miles west of the turnpike and roughly paralleling it from southwest to northeast, ran a low, wooded ridge that appeared virtually empty of hostile troops. If Jackson could seize that ridge, his men could sweep along its spine beyond the enemy's right flank, then swing down to the east and cut the Federal force off from Winchester. Colonel Samuel Fulkerson's brigade would lead the way, closely followed by the Stonewall Brigade minus its largest regiment, the 5th Virginia under Colonel William Harman, which would act as Jackson's reserve.

At about 3:30 the troops began to move along the cowpaths that crisscrossed the area. Fulkerson's brigade had formerly belonged to Loring and upon that officer's departure had been absorbed by Jackson. Fulkerson himself, as one of the ringleaders in the protest against Jackson, had much to make up for. Now he had his soldiers stepping smartly.

Artillery opened the battle. One Confederate battery sent a shell smashing into a barn filled with Federals. Jackson, riding by, clapped his hands and cried, "Good, good!"

Federal guns replied with unexpected strength, and under cover of the artillery duel Fulkerson's men ran for the key ridge. Brigadier General Garnett, coming up behind Fulkerson with his Stonewall Brigade, was already having problems: Orders that sometimes conflicted with his own were being sent by Jackson directly to regimental commanders.

Swarming onto the ridge, Fulkerson's regiments approached a clearing bisected by a stone wall. Just then Federals appeared at the far end of the field, and the two sides raced for the barrier. The Confederates won the race, crouching behind the wall and leveling a deadly fire at the onrushing enemy. The Federals fell back. Then another Federal regiment appeared out of the woods to the north and rushed toward the stone wall. It too was repulsed.

Observing from a nearby hill, Jackson was pleased — for a brief while. But enemy troops kept pouring out of the woods and, having twice been beaten back by the Confederate left, they now aimed their assault at

As the sun sets outside Kernstown, Virginia, the 84th Pennsylvania Regiment assaults the stone wall defended by two of Jackson's brigades, forcing the Confederates to

retire. But the cost was fearsome: Of the 300 Pennsylvanians making the assault, 109 were killed or wounded.

the center, where Garnett and the Stonewall Brigade had taken position in line with Fulkerson. Increasingly aware that he was facing no mere rear guard, Jackson belatedly sent an aide to reconnoiter. The officer soon reported that he estimated 10,000 Federals were on Jackson's front. "Say nothing about it," said Jackson. "We are in for it."

Pulling six regiments from his left, where Ashby clearly posed little threat, the Union's Colonel Kimball hurled wave after wave against the Stonewall Brigade, which held desperately to its line. This was fighting of the hardest sort, and it raged for better than two hours. But the Federals kept coming in seemingly endless numbers, and the Stonewall Brigade was running out of ammunition. In hopeless plight, Garnett awaited orders from Jackson. None arrived — for the commanding general was occupied elsewhere, trying to hurry his reserve, Harman's 5th Virginia, into the battle. At last, calculating that he had no other choice, Garnett passed word for the Stonewall Brigade to retire.

Heading back toward the front, Jackson was enraged to see retreating Confederates. Stopping one, he demanded: "Where are you going?" The man explained that he had run out of cartridges and did not know where to get more. Jackson's eyes blazed. "Then go back and give them the bayonet," he commanded.

Riding on, Jackson found Garnett. "Why have you not rallied your men?" he shouted. "Halt and rally!" Then he seized a drummer boy by the arm. "Beat the rally!" he cried. "Beat the rally!" Bravely the lad pounded his drum — without the slightest effect on the flood of men heading to the rear. Now the retreat was joined by Fulkerson's troops,

Brigadier General James Shields, who bested Stonewall Jackson at Kernstown, was a fiery Illinois politician who once challenged Abraham Lincoln to a duel over a newspaper article Lincoln had written. As Lincoln and Shields prepared to square off with cavalry sabers on a Mississippi River sand bar, their seconds reached a face-saving compromise.

who had been compelled to give way when their right flank was exposed by the withdrawal of the Stonewall Brigade.

Jackson had one more hope: Harman's 5th Virginia might yet drive back the enemy. But it was not to be. As Jackson later learned to his enduring displeasure, Garnett had ordered Harman to halt and form a line of battle to cover the Confederate retreat. In that assignment, Harman performed ably, holding the enemy at bay while Jackson collected his wounded. When his medical director warned that the task might take too long, Jackson replied: "Make yourself easy about that. This army stays here until the last wounded man is removed."

That evening, while Stonewall Jackson warmed himself at a campfire near Newtown, four and a half miles south of the battleground, he was approached by a soldier with more courage than sense. "The Yankees don't seem willing to quit Winchester, General," he said. Jackson replied tersely: "Winchester is a very pleasant place to stay in, sir." The youth persisted. "It was reported that they were retreating," he said, "but I guess they're retreating after us." Without turning his face from the fire, Jackson answered cryptically: "I think I may say I am satisfied, sir."

That sentiment was more than a little shaky, for the Valley army had suffered 718 casualties against 590 for the Union. General James Shields, recovering in a hospital five miles to the rear, could henceforth claim to be the only Federal commander ever to whip Stonewall Jackson.

By almost any standard, Jackson's performance at Kernstown had been imperfect. He had unquestioningly accepted Ashby's report, admittedly secondhand, of the enemy's weakness. He had thrown his tired troops into the fray without ordering or making an adequate reconnaissance. His tactics, although shrewdly conceived, were marred in execution by confused and even conflicting orders, and his reserve had arrived too late to turn the tide.

Yet despite Jackson's mistakes and shortcomings, the Battle of Kernstown had impressed Federal authorities with the fact that they were confronted in the Shenandoah Valley by a Confederate commander of rare and dangerous belligerency. Banks was recalled to the Valley, along with Alpheus Williams' division of 9,000 men. Beyond that, President Lincoln decided that if Jackson were bold enough to attack Shields, he would hardly hesitate to move against western Virginia, where Major General John C. Frémont had just taken command. Lincoln ordered that Brigadier General Louis Blenker's 10,000-man division be detached from McClellan's Army of the Potomac and sent to reinforce Frémont, pausing in the Valley to assist Banks if needed.

Such shifts added to a muddle that was already plaguing the Federals. Earlier in March a conference of McClellan's corps commanders, called at Lincoln's insistence, had determined that the safety of Washington required a garrison of 40,000 and a covering force at Manassas of 25,000 more.

The return of Banks to the Valley subtracted from the number available for the capital's defense, and the President ordered that General Irvin McDowell and his 40,000-man corps, which had been scheduled as the last of McClellan's units to embark for the Peninsula, remain around Manassas. Writing to McClellan, Lincoln explained: "I was satisfied with your arrangements to leave Banks at Manassas Junction, but when that arrangement was broken up and nothing was substituted for it of course I was not satisfied."

Finally, Lincoln removed the Valley district from McClellan's overall command, forestalling any claims that McClellan might make on the forces under Banks and leaving Banks answerable to the President himself. Clearly, Lincoln intended to become an active participant in the game of wits being played with Thomas Jackson in the Shenandoah Valley.

An Irregular War in Wild Terrain

The war on the flank of the Shenandoah Valley in southwestern Virginia was a deadly game of hide-and-seek. After a decisive Federal victory at Carnifex Ferry (*right*) in September 1861 and Federal occupation of the region, roving bands of Confederate irregulars launched a campaign of ambush and raiding west of the Alleghenies.

"Their methods outrivaled the savage," a Federal soldier claimed. "They would lie in wait until an opportunity presented itself to kill the party they sought. Then they would remain watching the corpse to kill the men who might come to bury it."

The Federals fought back with stratagems of their own. "The command became an army of scouts," an Ohio soldier recalled, "adopting perforce a system of independent warfare." The men traveled light, carrying only their weapons, ammunition, blankets, and perhaps some coffee and salt to trade with farmers in return for a hot meal and a place to sleep. Among the Federal soldiers was an artist from Cincinnati named John Roesler, who made these lithographs from his field sketches.

The patrolling was often a brutal business. "There was no sentiment in driving bushwackers from their lairs," a Federal soldier wrote. "They never made an open attack. A puff of smoke and the whiz of a bullet was the only warning."

When the weather turned too cold to fight, the irregulars simply returned to their farms and passed themselves off as pro-Union men. And the Federals retreated to their camps, where they faced long, lonely days of picket duty and drill before the next round of bushfighting.

Federal troops assault Confederate breastworks at Carnifex Ferry, a strategic crossing on the Gauley River. After nightfall brought to an end four hours of bitter fighting, the outnumbered Confederates withdrew across the river.

On patrol in Confederate territory, a detachment from the 47th Ohio Volunteers descends a steep forest trail in the Kanawha Valley region.

A Federal gun crew mans a howitzer on a crag known as Hawk's Nest, 1,200 feet above the New River, southwest of Carnifex Ferry. From this position, artillery men could command the river in both directions.

In a raging thunderstorm, a Federal patrol on Big Sewell Mountain reconnoiters a Confederate camp across a deep gorge. The awful weather prevented Federal forces from mounting an effective attack.

Federal troops at Miller's Ferry fire across the New River at Confederates hidden in the thick underbrush on the opposite shore. The Confederates fled when two Federal companies were dispatched across the river.

From a bluff overlooking the Gauley River, Federal pickets guard a hand-operated ferry linking the eastern shore with the supply depot and camp on the far bank. The three stone piers were all that remained of a wooden bridge wrecked by retreating Confederates.

"God Blessed Our Arms"

"We are the most timid and scrupulous invaders in all history. It must be delicious to the finer feelings of some people to watch our velvet-footed advance. It keeps me in a state of chronic contempt."

MAJOR WILDER DWIGHT, 2ND MASSACHUSETTS INFANTRY, NATHANIEL BANKS'S ARMY

After their defeat at Kernstown, Jackson and his Valley army spent three days retreating slowly, grudgingly, to the vicinity of Mount Jackson. There, before the tent stakes were firmly planted, the general summoned one of the army's most recent recruits, and in so doing, he took a small step that would help change the course of the Valley Campaign. The novice was Jedediah Hotchkiss. He was a 34-year-old schoolmaster, and his rare hobby was making maps.

Young Hotchkiss was a transplanted New Yorker. In 1847, while on a walking tour, he had become so enamored of the Shenandoah Valley that he decided to make it his home. He had begun tutoring children in Augusta County and was rewarded when local farmers took up a collection to help him start the Mossy Creek Academy. Later he founded another school. Both were successful.

In his spare time, Hotchkiss had taught himself the science of cartography, and in 1861 he put it to use. Although he opposed secession and detested slavery, his affections lay with the South, and he went to work as a civilian topographical engineer under General Robert E. Lee in northwestern Virginia. Soon he was invalided home with typhoid, but he recovered and hooked up with a militia regiment that joined the Valley army just three days before the battle of Kernstown.

By then Jackson had heard about Hotchkiss, and had thought about how to put his special talents to work. When Hotchkiss arrived at his headquarters on March 26, Jackson questioned him closely about his experience, and then gave a directive that would bring rich dividends. "I want you to make me a map of the Valley, from Harpers Ferry to Lexington, showing all the points of offense and defense," he said. Then, referring to his aide-de-camp, he added, "Mr. Pendleton will give you orders for whatever outfit you want. Good morning, sir."

Henceforth, as a captain on Jackson's staff, Jed Hotchkiss would prove invaluable. As events of the next several weeks would dramatically demonstrate, a thorough understanding of the region's topography was the key to military success in the Shenandoah Valley. With Jed Hotchkiss at his side, feeding him vital information about the Valley's roads, rivers, mountains and passes, Jackson was able to plan the maneuvers that would make his Valley Campaign a model for future generations of military men. Thanks to Hotchkiss, Jackson could almost always view his options realistically.

On the other hand, a Federal commander invading the Valley was a stranger in alien territory. He lacked reliable charts to guide him. His eyes were his inexperienced cavalrymen, many of them riding mediocre mounts. The Federal army would be nearly blind as it groped its way southward through the hostile Valley.

The Union's General Nathaniel Banks was quick to sense the dangers lurking ahead. After the victory at Kernstown, Banks had

Confederate General Richard Ewell wore this frock coat of heavy wool, cut in the style then favored by French Army officers. The three-button grouping on the front denotes Ewell's rank of major general.

followed Jackson only gingerly. In two days of pursuit, his advance units got no farther than Tom's Brook, a scant four miles south of Strasburg. There they were brought up short by Turner Ashby's horsemen on the far side of the little stream, and there Banks remained for a full week, trying to figure out the terrain, and complaining that Jackson's "pickets are very strong and vigilant."

Finally, on April 2, Banks's men slogged their way across Tom's Brook and plodded south. After a 10-mile march they arrived by nightfall at Stony Creek—only to find Ashby again on the other side. The position had been recommended to Jackson by Jedediah Hotchkiss, who had surveyed the area and found it a good one for a delaying action. Stony Creek was wide, with steep banks, and swollen by spring rains. And Turner Ashby had burned the only bridge across the stream.

Jackson and the main body of his army were waiting 10 miles to the south, outside Mount Jackson. There the Valley army had occupied Rude's Hill, a natural 100-foot-high bastion protected both to the west and the north by the North Fork of the Shenandoah, which made a sharp bend at that point. A single bridge spanned the river, and it could be destroyed in the event of a Federal breakthrough at Stony Creek.

Banks paused at Stony Creek to worry, just as he had done at Tom's Brook. Several difficulties were confronting him: Ashby remained aggressive; Stony Creek posed a substantial hazard; and the wretched early-April weather, with heavy rains and slushy snowfalls, was hardly conducive to military operations. And, despite the overwhelming numerical superiority of the Federal force, Banks was puzzled and worried by the nature of the land south of the stream. So, even while vowing to strike "an effective blow," Banks lingered north of Stony Creek for two weeks.

For Jackson, the interlude ushered in the most significant phase of the Valley Campaign. Back in early March, when General Joseph Johnston had been about to withdraw from Manassas, he had instructed Jackson to conform with the southward movement of Johnston's army, while blocking or at least delaying any attempt by Banks to join McClellan's forces north of the Rappahannock. But now, as Jackson established himself at Rude's Hill, the strategic situation was drastically changed. McClellan had transferred most of his command to the Peninsula, and on April 8 Johnston's main force fell back from the line of the Rapidan in order to oppose the huge Federal army's march toward Richmond.

Johnston, realizing that his movement left Jackson uncovered and isolated, had sent him new orders. Henceforth, the primary purpose of the Valley army should be to prevent Banks from taking the railroad town of Staunton, from which the Union could not only control the Shenandoah Valley but threaten the main supply line east to Richmond. To assist Jackson in this enterprise, Johnston had left behind an 8,500-man division near Brandy Station, east of the Blue Ridge. The division commander was a crusty old general named Richard S. Ewell, and at once he and Jackson began a correspondence about ways in which they might cooperate to confound the enemy.

What they did would obviously be dictated by the Valley's geography. And the hiatus provided by Banks's perplexed delay at Stony Creek gave Jackson plenty of time to lay plans according to the maps that cartographer Hotchkiss was supplying.

Crucial to operations in the Valley was the grid of roads that formed a rough parallelogram around the Massanutten. Running 80 miles north-south between Staunton and Winchester on the Massanutten's western side was the Valley Turnpike, the macadam marvel of its time, so straight that in places it offered a clear view ahead for two or three miles, and negotiable in all sorts of weather.

On the other side of the Massanutten, between it and the Blue Ridge, a much inferior road ran through the forested Luray Valley from Conrad's Store north to Front Royal. Another road skirted the northern end of the Massanutten, linking Front Royal to Strasburg and the Valley Turnpike. At the Massanutten's southern end, a rough track connected the turnpike near Harrisonburg with the Luray Valley road, then continued eastward across the Blue Ridge through Swift Run Gap to Stanardsville.

Along its entire length, the Massanutten was traversed by only one road. This ran from New Market up the western side of the ridge, and then descended to split into two branches. One fork continued east to the village of Luray, then passed through Thornton's Gap in the Blue Ridge to Sperryville; the other turned southeastward to Fisher's Gap. Rugged though it was, the route across the Massanutten was of critical strategic importance. Any troops marching north or south along either side of the Massanutten would be exposed to flank attack from an enemy holding the New Market-Luray passageway. Conversely, whichever army controlled this route could move with relative impunity along either the Valley Turnpike or the Luray Valley road.

The Master of Maps

"Had a hard day's duty, having ridden not less than thirty-five miles in rain and sleet, over rough mountain roads." Thus did Jedediah Hotchkiss describe in his diary a typical day as the mapmaker for Stonewall Jackson during the Valley Campaign.

Jackson relied heavily on his gifted young protégé. The general was a good enough judge of terrain when he stood on it, but his grasp of the Shenandoah Valley's complex topography was insufficient for planning a fast-paced campaign. Thus he was quick to appreciate and support Hotchkiss' work. "He furnished me with every facility that I desired for securing topographical information," the mapmaker wrote, "allowing me a complete transportation outfit for my exclusive use."

With his small escort, or sometimes alone, Hotchkiss scoured the countryside, gathering essential topographical data. Back in camp, he would often labor long into the night, converting his extensive notes into accurate maps. As the campaign gained momentum, Jackson came to depend more and more on Hotchkiss' maps. "Do not be afraid of making too many," he once told his cartographer.

CARTOGRAPHER JEDEDIAH HOTCHKISS

Using a transit compass, pocket compass and altimeter (*left to right*), Jedediah Hotchkiss made precise topographical readings from which he drew rough maps in his field sketchbook (*right*). Eventually he mapped the entire Valley.

This volume is my field sketch book that I used during the war. Most of the sketches were made on horseback just as they now appear. The colored pencils used were kept in the places fixed on the outside of the other cover.

These topographical sketches were often used in conferences with Generals Jackson, Ewell and Early.

The cover of this book is a blank Federal Commission found in Gen. Milroy's quarters at Winchester.

Jed. Hotchkiss

At his Rude's Hill redoubt, Jackson was situated just north of New Market. He therefore commanded the vital road across the Massanutten. And, in view of his orders from Johnston and his correspondence with Ewell, he saw several possibilities for action.

If Banks applied irresistible pressure, the Valley army could continue retreating southward on the turnpike, fighting as it went and hoping that the Federal advance might bog down before reaching Staunton. But this plan offered only a forlorn prospect.

The road across the Massanutten promised brighter options. On it, Jackson could take his army to Fisher's Gap or Thornton's Gap, and there, joined by Ewell, make a strong stand against any effort by Banks to dislodge him. Even if Banks were successful, the Confederates could escape across the Blue Ridge.

Jackson, however, anticipated that Banks would refuse to be lured into the mountains and would simply continue driving south toward Staunton. If that were the case, and if Jackson held the Massanutten pass, he might descend from the mountain and strike the Federal army's flank. Even more promising, he might use the Luray Valley as a covered corridor to march north, severing the enemy supply line — the Manassas Gap Railroad — at Front Royal. For that matter, he could swing around the northern end of the Massanutten and assault Banks from the rear.

The idea of moving north was alluring — but dangerous. If Banks were to seize the Massanutten passage and then place heavy forces at each end of the Luray Valley, the Valley army would be bottled up and would have no choice but to abandon the Shenandoah by way of the Blue Ridge.

There remained, however, another possible course. Trusting in his adversary to follow cautiously, Jackson could fall back to the southern end of the Massanutten, then hurry eastward to Conrad's Store. There, with his camp nestled between two protruding shoulders of the Blue Ridge, his flanks would be protected by dense forests, tangling vines and thorny thickets. To his front would lie the barrier of the South Fork; a Federal attack from that direction would require Banks to make a river crossing in the face of concentrated fire from Confederate cannon. On the improbable chance that such an assault was successful, Jackson, reinforced by Ewell, could defend the Blue Ridge heights at Swift Run Gap and, even if defeated, escape to the east.

Conrad's Store also presented offensive opportunities well suited to Jackson's tastes. There Jackson could thwart any Federal move up the Luray Valley. And if Banks were to venture south from Harrisonburg toward Staunton, Jackson would be in perfect position to assail the strung-out Federal flank. Of course, if Banks failed to exploit the road across the Massanutten and send a force east, the Luray Valley would remain open for a Confederate march northward.

As Jackson pondered these fascinating possibilities, Banks remained thoughtful and stationary, his army separated from Turner Ashby's thin line by Stony Creek. "Ashby still here," he informed Washington on the 15th of April. Then he added reassuringly, "We have a sleepless eye on him, and are straining every nerve to advance as quickly as possible."

Banks finally decided that his best course of action was to seize the crossroads at New Market. So, on April 16, Federal cavalry rode up Stony Creek, forded it at a place where Ashby's men had neglected to post pickets, and captured 60 surprised Confederate troopers. Before dawn the next day, Banks threw infantry across Stony Creek. Federal cavalry galloped across a wooden bridge that spanned the North Fork of the Shenandoah, driving off Ashby's troopers, who had made an amateurish effort to burn the bridge. The Confederate horsemen then had to fight their way back to Jackson's line at Rude's Hill.

Ashby, superb in battle, was among the last to reach the covering fire of Jackson's guns. No sooner had he arrived than his great white stallion, its gleaming coat now splotched with blood, fell dead of a bullet in its lungs. "Thus," wrote Jackson's young aide, Lieutenant Henry Kyd Douglas, "the most splendid horseman I ever knew lost the most beautiful war-horse I ever saw." By evening, Confederate souvenir collectors had plucked out all the hairs from the animal's mane and tail.

Although his artillery slowed the enemy drive, Jackson calculated that Banks's rare show of pugnacity meant that he had been heavily reinforced. Following his preferred plan, he abandoned the Rude's Hill position and headed south in a hurry. His army arrived in Harrisonburg on April 18. The next day it marched 20 miles to the east and camped that night near Conrad's Store at the foot of Swift Run Gap.

While Jackson was hurrying toward Conrad's Store, Banks occupied New Market. There he awakened to the strategic significance of the road that led from the town across the Massanutten. On April 19 he sent an expedition, whose strength Jackson estimated at 1,000 men, over the mountain to seize the Luray Valley bridges across the South Fork. The Federal force easily routed a band of Ashby's cavalrymen who had been sent to destroy the bridges but who had partaken liberally of the local applejack along the way.

By now, however, Banks had completely lost track of the Valley army. "I believe Jackson left this valley yesterday," he informed Secretary Stanton. Again, on April 22, he wired that "Jackson has abandoned the valley of Virginia permanently." Even so, he moved at a cautious pace, covering only 35 miles in 10 days. Not until April 26 was his main body assembled in Harrisonburg.

As usual, Banks completely misread the enemy's condition and intention. Earlier in April, he had reported that Jackson's force was "much demoralized by defeat, desertion, and the general depression of spirits. He is not in condition to attack, neither to make strong resistance." On April 28, Banks repeated himself: "The enemy is in no condition for offensive movements." And on April 30, he announced triumphantly that "there is nothing more to be done by us in the valley."

In that wrongheaded belief, Banks now requested that he and his army be transferred east of the Blue Ridge to join with either McClellan or McDowell for the march on Richmond. "I pray your favorable consideration," he wired Stanton. "Such order will electrify our force."

Banks got considerably less than he hoped for. Stanton, after consulting with President Lincoln, ordered on May 1 that General Shields's division should march to unite with General McDowell at Fredericksburg; upon the arrival of the Valley troops, McDowell with 40,000 men would move south to com-

As smoke rises from a bridge set afire by Turner Ashby's Confederate cavalrymen, a brigade of Banks's army sets off from the Federal camp at Strasburg in pursuit of the raiders. A Massachusetts officer wrote of Ashby in March 1862: "He is light, active, skilful, and we are tormented by him like a bull with a gadfly."

bine with McClellan's Peninsular army for a drive against the Confederate capital. Banks himself was assigned to stay in the Valley with a force now reduced to a single division.

Even though Lincoln and Stanton had at least partly accepted Banks's assurances of the Valley enemy's decrepitude, others remained doubtful. "What," queried Colonel George Gordon pointedly, "had become of Jackson?"

In fact, Jackson was still in his safe haven at Conrad's Store, and he was winding up some unpleasant household chores. This work he had begun on the road from Kernstown, when he directed that the Stonewall Brigade's commander, Richard Garnett, be relieved and placed under arrest for ordering a withdrawal.

Garnett's removal came as a stunning blow to the Stonewall Brigade. Garnett had trained and treated his men well, and was extremely popular with them. And their dismay was sharply increased by the arrival of the new commanding officer, Brigadier General Charles Sidney Winder, whom they found quite objectionable. Winder, 32 years old, was a West Pointer who had fought valorously against the Spokane Indians in Washington. But he was also a Maryland aristocrat and a stiff-backed commander who enforced regulations as strictly as Jackson did. "As he was a kind of fancy General," wrote Private John Casler, "and seemed to put on a good many airs, and was a very strict disciplinarian, the boys all took a dislike to him from the start, and never did like him afterwards."

But Winder won Jackson's gratitude by helping him settle a ticklish personal matter. The chilly Winder had, most improbably, struck up a friendship with Jackson's fiery cavalry commander, Turner Ashby. Thus, when relations between Jackson and Ashby reached an impasse that threatened to deprive the army of Ashby's services, Winder was able to act as a mediator.

In blood and in spirit, Colonel Ashby was a true descendant of the martial Virginians who had fought in the Revolution and the War of 1812. Like many another member of the cavalier society, his formal education had been neglected, but he was a marvelous horseman and a fine shot. He also thirsted to avenge the death of his brother Dick, a cavalry captain who in an early skirmish with Federals had been riddled with bullets and then bayoneted. Ever since, wrote a soldier who knew him, Turner Ashby would "quit a meal at anytime for a chance at a Yankee," and had "perhaps killed more of them with his own hand than any one man in the State."

Of slight but graceful physique, with swarthy skin, jet black hair and one of the army's most imposing beards, Colonel Ashby was indeed a fearless and spirited officer. Yet Jackson had discovered to his intense discomfort that Ashby was severely limited. To be sure, Ashby and his dashing horsemen had few peers at the hither and thither of guerrilla operations, and they were no less adept at the thrust and parry of rearguard fighting. But in the disciplines demanded for coordinated action with the rest of the army, Ashby's troopers were all but hopeless — and the fault clearly lay with their commander.

"He was without capacity or disposition to enforce discipline on his men," wrote a Confederate officer who otherwise much admired Ashby. In the Kernstown battle, for example, Ashby had managed to field only

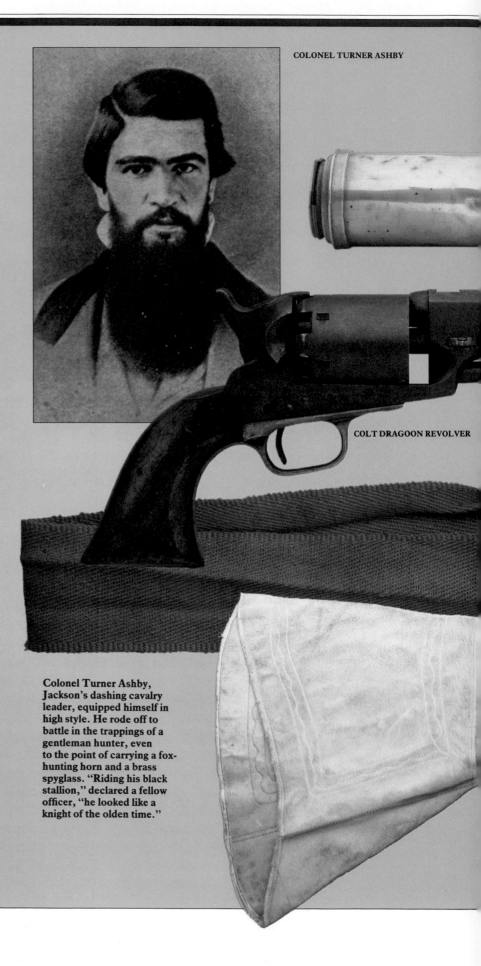

COLONEL TURNER ASHBY

COLT DRAGOON REVOLVER

Colonel Turner Ashby, Jackson's dashing cavalry leader, equipped himself in high style. He rode off to battle in the trappings of a gentleman hunter, even to the point of carrying a fox-hunting horn and a brass spyglass. "Riding his black stallion," declared a fellow officer, "he looked like a knight of the olden time."

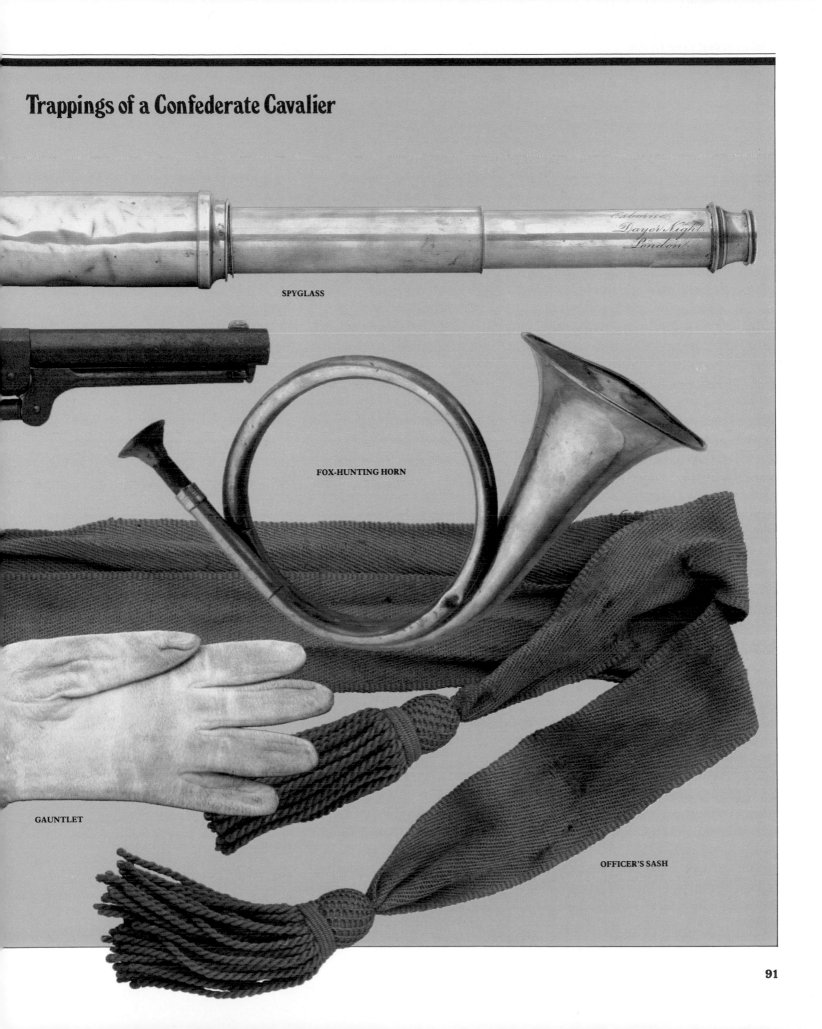

Trappings of a Confederate Cavalier

SPYGLASS

FOX-HUNTING HORN

GAUNTLET

OFFICER'S SASH

about 300 of his men, or less than half; the rest had been left free to gambol about the countryside on their own business because Ashby had thought that the issue would not be joined until the following day.

Since then, the situation had worsened, and Jackson came to the conclusion that he could no longer abide the continuing derelictions of his cavalry leader. Toward the end of April he issued a brief, blunt order: Ten of Ashby's 21 companies were to be attached to Winder's brigade, the rest to a brigade recently taken over by Brigadier General William B. Taliaferro. Ashby would be in charge of either the advance guard or the rear, but he could obtain the men necessary for carrying out his assignments only by applying to Generals Taliaferro and Winder for troops. In short, Ashby would be a commander without a command.

Upon receiving the order, Ashby stomped furiously into his headquarters, booted some shavings into a fire and sat morosely before the blaze. Were he and Jackson equal in rank, he insisted, he would instantly challenge his persecutor to a duel. But since he was barred from that satisfaction, he would instead take other action; Ashby and his second-in-command, Major Oliver Funsten, decided to resign.

Jackson had got himself into a pretty pickle. He could not pretend that the cavalry's performance would improve with the departure of its hero—an officer he valued for his fighting spirit and inspirational leadership. Jackson had meant to change Ashby, not to get rid of him.

Just as it appeared that Jackson's dilemma was beyond solution, help came in the person of Charles Winder, who in the midst of an unseasonable snowstorm rode back and forth between the two disaffected chieftains, negotiating for a meeting between them. Winder's efforts paid off, and on the evening of April 24, Ashby called upon Jackson in his headquarters tent.

Exactly what transpired was never disclosed, but the practical results were quite obvious. Although the cavalry companies remained technically under the infantry brigade commanders, they were in fact "detailed" back to Ashby. In effect, as Jackson's own quartermaster wrote, the dispute had been resolved "by Genl. Jackson backing square down."

With Ashby somewhat chastened, albeit unreformed, Jackson completed the shaping of a staff that would serve him admirably during the long marches and hard fights that lay ahead.

Among his most recent acquisitions was a new assistant adjutant general—in Civil War armies a post equivalent to that of chief of staff. He was the Reverend Dr. Robert L. Dabney, 42, an eloquent sermonizer who had been a professor of theology and ecclesiastical history at the Union Theological Seminary in Richmond. For such shining religious credentials, Jackson was perfectly willing to overlook Dabney's lack of military experience.

When Dabney was offered the rank of major, he protested his ignorance of military matters. Jackson replied: "You can learn." Giving way, Dabney asked when Jackson wished him to assume his new duties. Said Jackson, "Rest today and study the Articles of War, and begin tomorrow."

At first, the Reverend Major Dabney was an object of much derision as he rode about the regimental camps wearing a beaver hat and toting an umbrella. But he soon proved

Stonewall Jackson expected much of his staff, most of whom are included in this photographic display. Above all, their general demanded unhesitating obedience. Claimed Jackson's chief of staff, Major Robert Dabney (*upper right*), "If he found in an officer a hearty and zealous purpose to do all his duty, he was the most tolerant and gracious of superiors, overlooking blunders and mistakes with unbounded patience."

Lt Genl T. J. Jackson & Staff

Taken at Richmond, Va.

his inestimable worth, as the Valley army's parson, an able administrator and a soothing companion to Jackson—the two ate at the same table and frequently slept in the same room. Moreover, as one hard-bitten colonel pointed out: "Our parson is not afraid of Yankee bullets, and I tell you he preaches like hell."

Less conspicuous but perhaps even more valuable was Jackson's aide-de-camp, a brilliant 22-year-old captain named Alexander "Sandie" Pendleton. Pendleton, who had entered Washington College at the age of 13, produced clear and succinct written versions of Jackson's orders, dispatches free of the ambiguities that afflicted those of so many other commanders. The youngster's knowledge of army routine was such that on one occasion, when Jackson was asked about some obscure detail, the general replied, "Ask Sandie Pendleton. If he does not know, no one does."

Jackson also relied heavily on Hunter McGuire, his medical director. The General's first impression of McGuire was not good. The 25-year-old doctor had reported for duty in May of 1861 looking so young and frail that Jackson thought there must have been some mistake. He even contacted Richmond to verify the appointment. But Jackson soon came to respect McGuire. After the battle at Bull Run, the doctor treated Jackson's wounded hand and succeeded in saving a finger that another surgeon advised amputating. McGuire was also a talented administrator. He reorganized the medical service of the Valley army, made improvements in its ambulance corps and developed the first system of mobile field hospitals in the Confederacy.

Quartermaster John Harman was of much

rougher cut—and he stood as living proof that Jackson's deaconly instincts did not get in the way of his using a good man. In peacetime the owner and operator of a Valley stagecoach line, Major Harman possessed a vocabulary of curses and obscenities that was greatly admired by the troops. Recalled an officer: "Soldiers used to say he could start a mule train a mile long by his strong language at the back end."

The provisions that went into Harman's supply wagons were requisitioned by Major Wells J. Hawks, the army's commissary officer and altogether a quieter, less colorful sort than his teamster counterpart. Yet in his own way, Hawks was just as proficient as Harman. Apparently his talents included procuring the endless supply of lemons that Jackson sucked to relieve his dyspepsia. The soldiers speculated often on the source of the lemons but, unable to solve the mystery, they simply gave Hawks's trains the name "lemon wagons" and let it go at that.

In the blend of their separate skills and personalities, the men of Jackson's staff made an effective team. They were well able to face the tests that were pressed upon them by a general whom Jackson instinctively trusted beyond all others: Robert E. Lee.

Lee had a high-sounding title—Commanding General of Confederate Armies—but little if any authority. At most, he was military adviser to a President who had a notorious aversion to taking advice. In that capacity, Lee could not command; he could only suggest. And that, in a letter to Jackson dated April 21, is what he did.

Though fraught with significance for the future, the letter began almost routinely with the news that General Irvin McDowell had

Major General Richard S. Ewell was a great admirer of Jackson's tactical gifts, but often thought him reckless. Ewell confided to one of his staff officers that he "never saw one of Jackson's couriers approach without expecting an order to assault the North Pole."

moved to occupy Fredericksburg as a base of operations against Richmond. Then, in tentative terms, Lee wrote: "If you can use Genl. Ewell's division in an attack on Genl. Banks and to drive him back, it will prove a great relief to the pressure on Fredericksburg."

Jackson was eager to oblige, and on April 29 offered Lee a plan for taking the offensive. Jackson's proposal would involve the Valley army, Richard Ewell's division — now near Stanardsville — and a 2,800-man detachment under Brigadier General Edward Johnson, who had been holding out in the Alleghenies since the previous year. In recent days Johnson had been forced from his mountain positions by the Federals, and he was now being pressed close to Staunton by Brigadier General Robert H. Milroy,

who commanded the vanguard of John C. Frémont's army.

Under Jackson's scheme, General Ewell would cross the Blue Ridge and take over the Valley army's camps at Swift Run Gap. From there, Ewell could threaten Banks if he moved against Staunton. Meanwhile, Jackson would march to join Johnson just west of Staunton. The two could combine to defeat an outnumbered Milroy before the rest of Frémont's scattered army could come up, thereby forestalling a linkup between Frémont and Banks at Staunton. Finally, Jackson would combine his own command with those of Ewell and Johnson. Then, with an army of 17,000 men, by far the most he had ever possessed, Jackson could deal with General Banks.

Jackson informed Ewell of his plan and did not wait for Lee's answer. On the following night, April 30, Ewell's 8,500 men trudged over the Blue Ridge, picked their way in the darkness through General Jackson's slumbering camp and bivouacked a short distance beyond. Next morning, recalled one of the soldiers in Ewell's division, "to our utter amazement, when we turned our faces to where we had passed his army the evening previous, nothing met our gaze but the smouldering embers of his deserted campfires."

Jackson was gone, marching to the attack in the mist and rain that had descended upon the Valley of Virginia.

So began a dreadful ordeal for Richard Stoddert Ewell, who in the days ahead would be driven to distraction by the strange and secretive behavior of the Valley commander. By habit, Ewell was every bit as peculiar as Jackson; in appearance, he was a good deal more so. Wrote General Richard Taylor, one

Footsore and weary, Stonewall Jackson's troops nevertheless raise a cheer as they march past their commander on a spring day in the Shenandoah Valley in 1862.

of Ewell's brigadiers and a man with a gifted pen: "Bright, prominent eyes, a bomb-shaped, bald head, and a nose like that of Francis of Valois, gave him a striking resemblance to a woodcock; and this was increased by a bird-like habit of putting his head on one side to utter his quaint speeches."

A 44-year-old bachelor, Ewell was like Jackson in being a chronic dyspeptic, and although he was known to be a first-rate cook, his own diet was restricted to frumenty: a mixture of hulled wheat, milk, sugar, raisins and egg yolk. When he spoke, it was in a high, chirruping lisp, and his utterances were punctuated by a frightful succession of oaths. Ewell's nervous energies,

wrote Taylor, "prevented him from taking regular sleep, and he passed nights curled around a camp-stool, in positions to dislocate an ordinary person's joints."

Ewell's nerves were hardly soothed by the injunctions Jackson had left behind. Ewell was supposed to prevent Banks from moving toward Staunton, discourage any Federal attempts to depart from the Valley for the effort against Richmond — and, all the while, remain right where he was at Swift Run Gap. Almost every day brought new messages from Jackson, telling little about his own plans but admonishing Ewell to stay put.

Finally, Ewell's fragile temper snapped. "Colonel," he angrily piped to James A.

Nicknamed Jackson's "foot cavalry" because of their speed and endurance on the march, Valley infantrymen move swiftly across the countryside. "It was said by some of the boys who timed us," wrote one soldier, "that we once marched three miles in thirty-three minutes."

Walker, one of his regimental commanders, "did it ever occur to you that General Jackson is crazy?"

This was the same James Walker who had, as a cadet, challenged Professor Jackson to a duel. Now, however, he was older and mellower. "I don't know, General," he said judiciously. While allowing that Jackson was known as Fool Tom at the Virginia Military Institute, Walker said, "I do not suppose that he is really crazy."

"I tell you, sir, he is as crazy as a March hare," squeaked Ewell. "He has gone away, I don't know where, and left me here with instructions to stay until he returns. I tell you, sir, he is crazy, and I will just march my division away from here. I do not mean to have it cut to pieces at the behest of a crazy man."

A few days later, Ewell heard that Jackson had been in a battle west of Staunton. Still, his orders required him to wait, and so he did — fretfully. On May 11, he learned from a prisoner that Shields's division was leaving Banks and the Valley. Ewell decided to send a regiment under Colonel Thomas T. Munford to try to delay the Federals.

Before he departed, Munford went to see Ewell, who was in bed. Ewell asked Munford to hand him a map, the colonel wrote later, "and with the aid of a miserable lard lamp he attempted to show me where General Jackson was. Before I knew what he was after, he sprang out of bed, with only a nightshirt on — no carpet on the floor — and down on his knees he went; his bones fairly rattled. His bald head and long beard made him look more like a witch than a major-general."

Feverishly pointing out the widespread Federal dispositions on the map, Ewell delivered a baffling diatribe against Jackson:

"This great wagon-hunter is after a Dutchman, the old fool! General Lee at Richmond will have little use for wagons if all of these people close in around him; we are left out here in the cold. This man Jackson is certainly a crazy fool, an idiot."

Then, thrusting into the astounded Munford's face a communiqué in which Jackson had told of capturing General Milroy's wagon train with the help of God, Ewell exploded: "What has Providence to do with Milroy's wagon train?"

Two days later, on May 13, Ewell wrote to a niece: "I have spent two weeks of the most unhappy I ever remember. I have a bad headache, what with the bother and folly of things. I never suffered as much from dyspepsia in my life. As an Irishman would say, 'I'm kilt entirely.' "

Jackson and the Valley army had emerged, meanwhile, from the wilderness of the Alleghenies after an adventuresome journey.

Leaving Swift Run Gap on the afternoon of April 30, the army had moved southwestward on a dirt road that ran along the east bank of the South Fork to the town of Port Republic. Marching in a downpour, the troops made only five miles before nightfall.

The next day was much worse. To veterans, the march was reminiscent of the awful trek to Romney — except that snow and ice had been replaced by rain and mud.

Under a lashing torrent, the track became a quagmire. Marching men sank to their knees; wagons and gun carriages were mired to their axles; struggling horses had to be pried from the muck with fence rails.

As rain continued to pelt the miserable men, Jackson himself pitched in to carry fence rails and stones for filling the mud holes. Still, the army bogged down after another five miles. Private Joe Kaufman, a new recruit, wrote in his diary: "I begin to think Old Jack is a hard master from the way he is putting us through. Oh, how I wish peace would be declared!"

The next day, May 2, the sun came out, but the mud remained. Jed Hotchkiss was sent ahead with an entire regiment as a work crew to try to shore up the road. Conditions, wrote Hotchkiss, were "the worst I ever saw in the Valley of Virginia."

In late afternoon Jackson's men finally neared Port Republic, but instead of crossing the Shenandoah River bridge that led to the town, they were ordered to turn east toward the Blue Ridge. The miserable troops slept that night at the western foot of Brown's Gap. In two and a half days of hard marching, the Valley army had progressed a mere 15 miles.

The 3rd of May dawned a lovely spring day, yet spirits were low as the men labored up the steep inclines of Brown's Gap, heading toward Charlottesville on the other side of the mountains. To their mystification and discontent, they were leaving the Shenandoah Valley without a fight.

Another surprise awaited the troops. On Sunday, May 4, as they arrived at Mechum's River Station, a stop on the Virginia Central line 10 miles west of Charlottesville, the men found Jackson already weeding out the sick and the lame. The healthy were packed into railroad baggage cars — which they supposed would carry them to Richmond and to the aid of General Joseph Johnston.

But when the trains pulled out they were heading not east toward Richmond but westward over the Blue Ridge, back to the Valley that had only yesterday been abandoned.

Federal General Robert Milroy, outmanned by Jackson at McDowell, launched a pre-emptive attack. Wrote a Confederate officer: "Milroy maintained the fight in the most spirited manner until dark, and in this way saved himself from disaster."

At McDowell on May 8, Jackson deployed his troops atop Sitlington's Hill in a wedge, with the 12th Georgia at the vertex. Federal infantry under Milroy repeatedly stormed the hill, but failed to dislodge the defenders. As night fell, the Federals retreated across the Bull Pasture River.

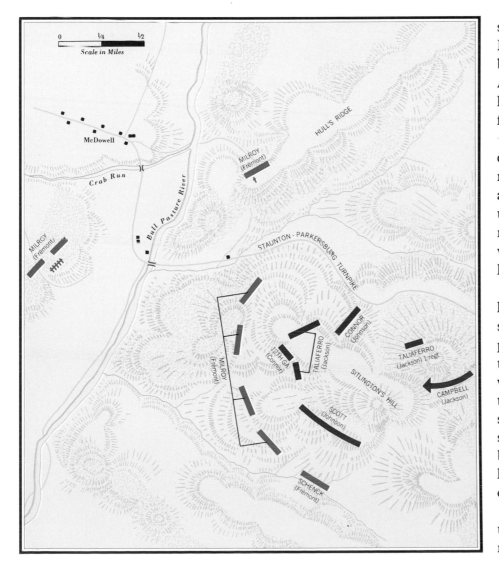

The whole heartbreaking exercise had been an elaborate charade — perhaps the first time in history that railroads were used for a military deception — designed by Jackson to trick his enemy into thinking he had departed the Valley for good.

That afternoon Jackson arrived in Staunton, which was in a panic over rumors that the army was giving up the Valley. Ashby's cavalry was already screening Staunton from Banks, whose army was still at Harrison-burg. To maintain strict secrecy, Jackson set up picket lines to halt all traffic out of Staunton; civilians from the surrounding country-side, who had come into town to see relatives and friends in the returning army, were barred from going home.

By the evening of May 5, Jackson's entire army was camped around Staunton. Only six miles to the west were General Edward Johnson's six regiments, withdrawing under pressure from Milroy's Federal troops.

On May 7, having heard from scouts and spies the surprising news that Jackson and Edward Johnson were combining against him, Milroy began to fall back toward the Alleghenies along the Staunton-Parkersburg highway. Johnson, who was spoiling for a fight, went after him.

Jackson got his own troops on the road early on the morning of May 7. While his regiments marched westward, Jackson rode ahead and caught up with Johnson's rear units on the eastern slopes of the Alleghenies. There, on the 8th of May, Jackson was taken in hand by Jed Hotchkiss, who had been with Johnson.

Hotchkiss escorted the general over the huge hump of Bull Pasture Mountain and, shortly before they reached the end of the precipitous descent, led him off to the left through a narrow gorge. Choked though it was with boulders and brush, the defile was the only negotiable route onto an isolated spur called Sitlington's Hill. Atop that steep-sided ridge was a mile-long plateau, broken by ravines and studded with sharply rising hillocks. There Edward Johnson was already deploying his infantry.

Johnson was a rough customer, a large, unkempt man with a bellowing voice and a nervous tic that made one eye wink constantly. He loved a brawl, and for that Jackson was happy to have him on the scene.

As the two generals faced westward from Sitlington's Hill, they saw 500 feet beneath them the rain-swollen Bull Pasture River. Beyond the stream on the flat surface of the flood plain, hemmed in on all sides by towering mountains, lay the village of McDowell—crowded with Federal troops. Approximately 500 yards west of the Bull Pasture River, on a ridge running roughly parallel to Sitlington's Hill, Federal artillery was in place.

The Confederates seemed clearly to hold the advantage. After months of trying, Jackson had at last brought together a numerically superior force against a Federal detachment. If both sides got all their men into action, Jackson would pit nearly 10,000 against Milroy's 6,000, including reinforcements under Brigadier General Robert C. Schenck, who had just arrived at McDowell and, being senior, had assumed command. Moreover, from their dominant position on Sitlington's Hill, Jackson's artillery could presumably sweep clean both the town of McDowell and the Federal-held ridge that lay beyond.

There was a hitch, however. The gorge that provided Jackson's only access to Sitlington's Hill was too rough to permit the passage of artillery—and thus Jackson lost his main advantage. Ordering Johnson to remain on the hill, he descended to deploy his arriving troops for an attack across the Bull Pasture River.

Schenck and Milroy knew nothing of the hitch in Jackson's plans. They did know from the reports of scouts that they were outnumbered. And when the scouts told them that Confederate guns were headed for

Sitlington's Hill, the Federal commanders judged that retreat was inevitable.

But they had to buy time — if the Confederates succeeded in placing cannon on Sitlington's Hill, the retreating Federal columns would be decimated. To prevent that, Milroy, who was in the words of Schenck a man of "impetuous, though rather uncalculating, bravery," suggested a pre-emptive assault. It might keep the Confederates pinned down until nightfall and enable the bulk of the Federal troops to get away under cover of darkness. Schenck approved, and shortly after 4:30 p.m., two thousand Federal troops, having crossed the Bull Pasture River on a bridge concealed from view by woods, came charging hard up Sitlington's Hill (map, page 101).

In Jackson's absence, the defense of the hill was in Edward Johnson's hands, and he had all he could manage. The first Federal rush almost broke the Confederate right. But Jackson, hearing the crackle of gunfire, rushed up Taliaferro's infantry, and the right flank held.

Then the Federals struck at Johnson's most vulnerable point — the center, where a Confederate wedge pointed toward the attacking enemy, exposing the defenders both to frontal and oblique fire.

The imperiled sector was manned by the 12th Georgia. The 12th was the only non-Virginia regiment on the Confederate side, and it meant to show its worth. When ordered to pull back to a more defensible line, the Georgians refused. Instead, they stood up, the better to fire down at the enemy climbing the hill. But now the Georgians, silhouetted against the sky, made perfect targets, and they took heavy losses. In spite of

the casualties, the Georgia line held. Next day, when asked why the regiment had defied orders, one of the Georgians replied: "We did not come all this way to Virginia to run before Yankees."

There was nothing fancy about this battle; it was a furious little slugging match. At the peak of the fighting, Edward Johnson went down with a mangled ankle. With Jackson still away bringing up his troops, command of the battlefield passed to General Taliaferro, who had something to prove. As one of the figures in the bitter dispute after Romney, he had earned Jackson's wholehearted hostility. When Taliaferro was subsequently assigned to the Valley army, Jackson had protested vehemently, but to no avail. Now, Taliaferro's reaction showed that he possessed considerable pluck. "I determined to do my duty," he wrote later, "and let him judge of me by my subsequent actions."

Taliaferro meant to fight his way into Jackson's good graces, and the battle of McDowell gave him his chance. He acquitted himself well. Throwing in the Valley army's 2nd Brigade as soon as it arrived on the scene, Taliaferro managed to hold Sitlington's Hill until, at about 9 p.m., darkness forced an end to the fighting. The Federals sullenly retired to McDowell. Next morning they were gone.

In the fight, Jackson had suffered 498 casualties, about one third of them from the 12th Georgia, against Milroy's 256. Yet he had forced the enemy from the field and effectively prevented any linkup at Staunton between Banks and Frémont. This outcome Jackson reported characteristically to Richmond: "God blessed our arms with victory at McDowell yesterday."

Soldiers of the Valley

"A fierce spirit animates these rough-looking men," declared a member of General Joseph Johnston's staff in May 1861 after reviewing a contingent of Confederate volunteers from the Shenandoah Valley. "If called upon, even now, to meet the enemy, I have no fear of the result."

The officer's assessment of these raw but self-reliant country folk was prophetic. Soldiers of the Valley, some of whom are portrayed on the following pages, would form the backbone of Stonewall Jackson's legendary Army of the Shenandoah and earn a reputation for invincibility among their Federal foe. Although many of them were still in their teens, all were outdoorsmen, riders and shooters in the robust physical condition that Jackson's rigorous notions of warfare demanded.

These hearty sons of immigrant pioneers saw the War in simple terms — they were fighting for their farms and villages against an alien invader. Valley people, said a Virginian, were "good lovers, good haters, unfaltering in courage, immovable in their convictions." When War came, the kith and kin of entire communities went off to fight together. One company of the 5th Virginia Infantry counted 18 members of a single family, and another outfit had six brothers.

Discipline was not among the soldierly assets of these troops. "We were ever ready to fight," a Valley recruit said, "but never ready to submit to the routine duty of the camp or the march." Despite Jackson's authoritarian efforts, the soldiers routinely ambled off on unauthorized furloughs to tend to chores at their farms, straggled from the columns to accept a hot dinner and a good night's rest from an adoring citizenry, sneaked into off-limits towns to court girls and cadge forbidden whiskey. "The truth is, we were soldier boys," a veteran recalled years later. "And the boy was sometimes more in evidence than the soldier."

This freewheeling approach to soldiering carried over to the battlefield, where as one man claimed, "every private was a general and needed no guidance or direction from his officer." In a charge, Valley troops rarely maintained the shoulder-to-shoulder line prescribed in the military manuals; their version, in the words of a Confederate general, was "more of a freelance than a machine," with each man racing forward, screaming like a banshee and firing as he saw fit.

Yet these untameable amateurs could march 36 miles a day in freezing weather on an empty stomach, engage a numerically superior enemy — and win. Valley men, a Confederate wrote, would have followed Stonewall Jackson "into the jaws of death itself. Nothing could have stopped them and nothing did."

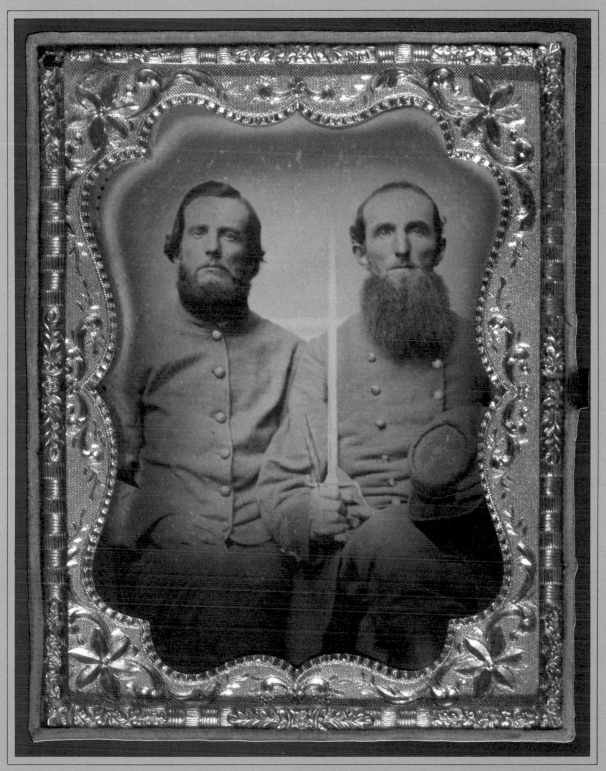

FATHER AND SON, 13TH VIRGINIA INFANTRY

PRIVATE MICHAEL BOWMAN, 7TH VIRGINIA CAVALRY

CADET JOHN T. D. GISINER

PRIVATE PETER L. KURTZ, 5TH VIRGINIA INFANTRY

SERGEANT GEORGE W. KURTZ, 5TH VIRGINIA INFANTRY

UNIDENTIFIED PRIVATE, 21ST VIRGINIA INFANTRY

LIEUTENANT EDWARD C. SHEPHERD, 2ND VIRGINIA INFANTRY

UNIDENTIFIED ARTILLERY PRIVATE

PRIVATE STEPHEN HANNAS, 7TH VIRGINIA CAVALRY

To Winchester and Beyond

"A flash, a report and a whistling bullet from some covert met us, but there were few casualties. I remember thinking at the time that Jackson was invulnerable, and that persons near him shared that quality."

BRIGADIER GENERAL RICHARD TAYLOR, THE LOUISIANA BRIGADE

General Richard S. Ewell could bear the maddening delay no longer. For three exasperating weeks, he had twiddled his thumbs at Swift Run Gap on the eastern shoulder of the Blue Ridge, puzzling and fuming over a series of instructions from his superiors. By the 16th of May, Ewell had received no fewer than 27 dispatches — from Jackson, who was off winning his small victory at McDowell, from Lee and from Johnston. Now he had had enough.

On May 13, Jackson had ordered Ewell to pursue General Nathaniel P. Banks's Federal army if Banks elected to withdraw down the Valley. According to the reports of cavalry scouts, Banks was already at Strasburg, the hub of the Manassas Gap Railroad in the central Valley. But Ewell's most recent order from General Johnston explicitly stated that if Banks's forces moved eastward across the Blue Ridge to link up with the Federal contingent under General Irvin McDowell at Fredericksburg, Ewell was to follow to reinforce Johnston. Ewell's cavalry had reported that General James Shields's 11,000-man division, more than half of Banks's total force of 18,600, was already on the march across the Blue Ridge. What should he do?

Ewell vowed not to wait for any more couriers. He ordered a horse, and in the early-morning darkness of May 18, set off at a gallop for Jackson's headquarters, 30 miles to the west near the town of Mount Solon.

The sun was just rising when Ewell came thundering into the Valley army's encampment. It was a soft Sunday morning, and Jackson's men were enjoying their first day off after marching 200 miles over the past 18 days. While the men sat in small groups preparing breakfast, the two generals went into conference in an old gristmill along a creek.

Jackson and Ewell spread their maps over the sacks of flour stacked on the floor and began to study the positions of the opposing forces. Both men knew what was at stake. At that very moment, Richmond was in danger from a powerful Federal pincer. Just 30 miles east of the Confederate capital was General George McClellan's Army of the Potomac, more than 105,000 strong. To the north of Richmond was McDowell's 40,000-man army.

The Confederate situation looked bleak indeed, but both Jackson and Ewell saw a dazzling opportunity. Since Shields's division had left the Shenandoah Valley to reinforce McDowell, Banks was now isolated and undermanned, with but 10,000 troops. The Federals had given Jackson the very opportunity he had schemed to create — by joining forces with Ewell, Jackson would outnumber his foe by nearly 2 to 1. If he moved fast enough, he could crush Banks.

But what to do about Johnston's orders to follow the Federals if they left the Valley? An order was an order. When Ewell maintained that he had no choice but to pursue Shields, Jackson seemed stunned. "Then Providence denies me the privilege of striking a blow for

These smoothbore 6-pounder cannon of Virginia's elite Rockbridge Artillery supported Stonewall Jackson throughout his Valley Campaign. The soldiers who manned the guns named them Matthew, Mark, Luke and John because, according to one account, "they spoke a powerful language."

my country," he replied, bitterly adding, "and I must be satisfied with the humble task of hiding my little army about these mountains, to watch a superior force."

Then Jackson grasped at a straw. He showed Ewell a letter from Lee dated May 16. Lee shared Jackson's strategic thinking, and although he had no command authority, his opinions still carried weight.

"Whatever may be Banks's intention," Lee had written, "it is very desirable to prevent him from going either to Fredericksburg or the Peninsula. A successful blow struck at him would delay, if it does not prevent, his moving to either place." After warning Jackson to be prepared should Johnston suddenly order him to rush to the defense of Richmond, Lee advised: "Whatever movement you make against Banks do it speedily, and if successful, drive him back towards the Potomac, and create the impression as far as practicable that you design threatening that line."

For weeks, the doughty Ewell had been aching for a fight. As the two generals pondered the dilemma, Ewell made his decision. So long as he remained in the Valley, he asserted, he was within Jackson's immediate jurisdiction. They must seize the opportunity. He would ignore Johnston's orders and obey Jackson's.

Straight away, Jackson ordered Ewell to write him a letter spelling out the dilemma. Jackson responded on paper immediately, in a way intended to absolve Ewell of any subsequent charges of disobedience. Jackson wrote Ewell:

"Your letter of this date, in which you state that you have received letters from Generals Lee, Johnston and myself requiring somewhat different movements, and desiring my views respecting your position, has been received. In reply I would state that as you are in the Valley District you constitute part of my command. Should you receive orders different from those sent from these headquarters, please advise me of the same at as early a period as practicable.

"You will please move your command as to encamp between New Market and Mount Jackson on next Wednesday night, unless you receive orders from a superior officer and that of a date subsequent to the 16th instant."

Their conference concluded, Jackson invited his guest to accompany him to the worship service to hear a sermon by the Reverend Major Robert Dabney. Although the irreverent Ewell was no churchgoer, he willingly accepted. As it happened, Dabney's text was taken from Matthew 11, verse 28: "Come unto me, all ye that travel and are heavy laden, and I will give you rest." It was a pleasant notion for the tired troops, but oddly inappropriate for the two generals.

No sooner had the services ended than Ewell leaped onto his horse and went galloping back toward Swift Run Gap to get his troops on the road. As for Jackson, the order went out to the Valley army to be ready to move at 5 a.m. the next day, May 19.

So began 10 days of marching and fighting that would make Stonewall Jackson a legend in his own time. His offensive would take him almost to the banks of the Potomac — and send a stab of fear through the Federal administration.

As the men of the Valley army hurried northward through Harrisonburg, they were told to store their knapsacks. "We knew there was some game at hand then," wrote Private John Casler, "for when General Jackson ordered knapsacks to be left behind he meant business."

On the afternoon of May 20, Jackson's troops encamped outside New Market, near the junction of the Valley Turnpike and the road running east across the Massanutten to the Luray Valley and the Blue Ridge.

Shortly after Jackson established his New Market headquarters, Ewell rode up. He had, as Lieutenant Henry Kyd Douglas described it, "ill humor on his face."

"General Ewell," cried Jackson with rare warmth, "I'm glad to see you. Get off!"

"You will not be so glad when I tell you what brought me," replied Ewell.

"What — are the Yankees after you?"

"Worse than that," said Ewell. "I am ordered to join General Johnston."

Just that morning, Ewell had received peremptory orders from Johnston dated May 17, forbidding an attack on Banks and requiring Ewell's immediate departure from the Shenandoah Valley.

It was stunning news. Stonewall Jackson had come too far, his opportunity was too great and his hopes were too high to be thwarted now. Risking a charge of insubordination, he suspended the execution of

Tall, burly and fearless, Confederate Major Chatham Roberdeau Wheat (*left*) was well suited to command the Louisiana Tigers, a battalion of wharf rats and ex-convicts from the New Orleans area. "It required the iron hand of discipline, tempered with fatherly kindness, to make soldiers of them," wrote a Confederate officer. "Wheat had these two good qualities in a remarkable degree." A drummer boy (*right*) displays the exotic Zouave garb worn by the Louisiana Tiger Rifles, one of Wheat's companies.

Johnston's order and fired off a telegram to Robert E. Lee: "I am of the opinion that an attempt should be made to defeat Banks, but under instructions just received from General Johnston I do not feel at liberty to make an attack. Please answer by telegraph at once."

Ewell rode back to his camp; there was nothing for Jackson to do but await an answer from Lee. And while he was contemplating the discouraging turn of fortune, the attention of his army was riveted upon the arrival of some outlandish strangers.

Northward down the Valley Turnpike, in neat gray uniforms with white gaiters flashing to the cadence of their march, beneath banners adorned with pelicans and behind blaring regimental bands, strode the 3,000

men of Ewell's largest brigade. They came from Louisiana — New Orleans dock workers, sugar plantation aristocrats and Acadians from the land of Evangeline. The most extraordinary of them all were the self-styled "Tigers," tough veterans of the Battle of Bull Run, a battalion of cutthroats, thieves and other rowdies taken from the alleyways of the mean towns that lined the banks of the lower Mississippi.

Ordered to join Jackson at New Market, the Louisiana Brigade had left the rest of Ewell's command at Conrad's Store near Swift Run Gap, skirted the southern extremity of the Massanutten and then turned north, making good time. Now orders to halt were snapped out in French — "gobble talk," as it was quickly labeled by the astounded Valley men who lined the turnpike — the Louisianians broke ranks, the bands played and many of the newcomers joined in pairs, clasping each other about the waist to dance in madcap abandon.

While the Valley army was gawking, the commander of the rollicking brigade sought out Jackson, whom he had never met. Richard Taylor was the son of General and later President Zachary Taylor and a brother-in-law, by virtue of his sister's marriage, to Confederate President Jefferson Davis. He was a frail man, this brigadier general from Louisiana, with dandified mannerisms. At 36, he was richly educated — at Harvard, Yale and Scotland's Edinburgh — yet his pre-Civil War military training had been limited to a visit to his father's border camp during the Mexican War. It was widely — and correctly — believed of Richard Taylor that he had attained his high military rank through his family connections. Even so, he was a natural soldier.

Taylor was a disciplinarian after Jackson's own heart. Shortly after he assumed command of the Louisiana Brigade, some of the unruly Tigers raided the guardhouse in a futile attempt to free their incarcerated comrades. The raiders were arrested, and a few hours later, two of the ringleaders were tried by court-martial and sentenced to death before a firing squad comprised of their fellow Tigers.

At that point the commander of the Tigers, Major Chatham Roberdeau Wheat, asked that the ugly task of execution be assigned to some other outfit. Wheat, the burly giant who had been terribly wounded in the Battle of Bull Run, generally got his way. Yet Taylor turned him down cold, and the sentence against the miscreants was carried out by other Tigers in full view of the assembled brigade. As an example of discipline, Taylor wrote later, "punishment, so closely following offense, produced a marked effect."

More often, Taylor's regimen took benign forms. For example, to cure straggling, he had insisted that the men bathe their feet in cold water at the end of each day's march; he taught them how to treat foot sores and blisters, and advised them how to select properly fitting boots and shoes. "Before a month had passed," recalled Taylor, "the brigade learned how to march."

Thus, as he sought out Jackson to introduce himself, Taylor was filled with pride at the marching abilities and sharp appearance of his men. What he saw in Jackson was less impressive.

Taylor related that the officer who was guiding him "pointed out a figure perched on the topmost rail of a fence overlooking the road and field, and said it was Jackson. Approaching, I saluted and declared my name

117

Warned by an outrider to slow down, a Federal Army teamster struggles to rein in his mules as his supply wagon lurches down a steep track in the Shenandoah Valley.

With rare exceptions, such as the paved Valley Turnpike, Shenandoah roads were only dirt paths — awash with mud after a rain, full of treacherous ruts when dry.

and rank, then waited for a response. Before this came I had time to see a pair of cavalry boots covering feet of gigantic size, a mangy cap with visor drawn low, a heavy, dark beard, and weary eyes."

Sucking on a lemon, Jackson gently asked how far Taylor's men had marched that day, and by what route.

"Keazletown road," responded Taylor. "Six and twenty miles."

"You seem to have no stragglers," observed Jackson.

"Never allow straggling."

"You must teach my people," said Jackson. "They straggle badly."

Just then one of Taylor's bands struck up a waltz, to which his men began dancing. After watching in silence for several moments, Jackson remarked: "Thoughtless fellows for serious work."

Taylor replied that he hoped "the work would not be less well done because of the gayety." Jackson said nothing and that was the end of the interview. But before very long Taylor would be given ample opportunity to show that his men could do a lot more than dance.

That same day, Jackson's urgent appeal to Lee was being considered in Richmond. Lee may have taken the matter directly to President Davis. At any rate, the anxiously awaited message authorizing an attack on Banks arrived from Richmond, and in the gray dawn of May 21, Jackson's men assembled in marching order with Taylor's brigade in the vanguard.

They started toward the north, heading down the Valley pike, as if to attack Banks at Strasburg. But as the men marched down Congress Street in the center of New Mar-

In a dispatch dated May 21, 1862, Confederate General Joseph E. Johnston gives Generals Jackson and Ewell guarded permission to join forces in the Valley against Federal troops under Nathaniel Banks.

ket, Jackson waved for a right turn onto Cross Street—toward the east on the road leading across the Massanutten. After a day's hard climb in sultry heat, they descended the eastern slope of the massif, crossed the South Fork of the Shenandoah and neared the village of Luray, where they were to camp for the night.

Richard Taylor, unaccustomed to his new leader's penchant for deception, was mystified. He had, after all, marched his men over the Massanutten only to recross the ridge and arrive at a place just 18 miles due north of Conrad's Store, his starting point. "I began to think," Taylor wrote wryly, "that Jackson was an unconscious poet, and, as an ardent lover of nature, desired to give strangers an opportunity to admire the beauties of his Valley."

The rest of Ewell's division was already encamped at Luray, and with it Jackson now had more than 16,000 men and 48 guns. As the combined forces started out early the next morning, May 22, the men still did not know their destination. Jackson could either cross the Blue Ridge through Thornton's Gap, thereby abandoning the Shenandoah Valley, or he could move north, screened by mountains on either side, to Front Royal, where a Federal detachment was deployed.

He took the road to Front Royal.

The army moved briskly. Jackson, impressed by the performance of Taylor's ranks, imposed a new set of marching rules. Henceforth the men marched for precisely 50 minutes of each hour; at the end of that time they halted, stacked arms and rested for exactly 10 minutes before moving out again. The brief but regular respites reduced straggling.

On this day's march, another new order that came down removed all doubt from the minds of Jackson's and Ewell's men that they were heading straight for a fight: Jackson decreed that only two men from each battalion, assigned to tend to the wounded and directed to wear identifying red badges on their caps, would be permitted to leave ranks during a battle.

That night Jackson halted 10 miles short of Front Royal.

Only 20 miles from Jackson's camp, General Nathaniel Banks was getting edgy. The prevailing atmosphere in Strasburg was hostile enough to make anyone nervous — a chaplain for the Union described the place as the "dirtiest, nastiest, meanest, poorest, most shiftless town I have yet seen in all the shiftless, poor, mean, nasty, dirty towns of this beautiful valley."

And Banks himself was painfully aware that his once imposing command had been sadly diminished and dispersed. He had lost 11,000 men with the departure of Shields. Aside from numerous small detachments guarding the line of the Manassas Gap Railroad, Banks had stationed 850 infantry and 600 cavalry at Winchester, two infantry companies of about 100 men at Buckton, between Strasburg and Front Royal, and — at Front Royal itself — 1,100 men of the 1st Maryland Regiment under Colonel John R. Kenly. That left Banks with little more than 7,600 men to defend the earthworks he was hastily building at Strasburg.

Moreover, one of Banks's ablest subordinates had questioned the wisdom of the Federals even trying to defend Strasburg. Colonel George H. Gordon, Banks's outspoken brigade commander, had pointed out that the Federal force at Strasburg might easily be cut off from its escape route to the east by the enemy, and had urged Banks to shift his troops to Winchester. But Banks, said Gordon, was immovable.

Still, Banks was concerned enough to seek reinforcements from Secretary of War Stanton. On May 22 he warned Stanton of "the persistent adherence of Jackson to the defense of the valley and his well-known purpose to expel the Government troops," and concluded: "There is probably no one more fixed and determined purpose in the whole circle of the enemy's plans."

Banks was wasting his time — Stanton and Lincoln were far too preoccupied with the impending offensive against Richmond to pay much attention to the Shenandoah Valley. On the very day of Banks's request, they had received a brief but electrifying message from General McDowell near Fredericksburg: "Major General Shields' command

A Spy in the Shenandoah

When Stonewall Jackson led the attack on Front Royal in May 1862, he had the advantage of knowing that only about 1,000 Federal soldiers defended the town. That fact had been supplied to him by a 17-year-old Confederate spy named Belle Boyd (*right*).

Belle Boyd's career in espionage began by chance. On the Fourth of July, 1861, a band of drunken Federal soldiers broke into her home in Martinsburg, intent on raising the U.S. flag over the house. When one of them insulted her mother, Belle drew a pistol and killed him. A Federal board of inquiry exonerated her, but sentries were posted around the house and officers kept close track of her activities. She profited from this enforced familiarity, charming at least one of the officers, Captain Daniel Keily, into revealing military secrets. "To him," she wrote later, "I am indebted for some very remarkable effusions, some withered flowers, and a great deal of important information." Belle conveyed those secrets to Confederate officers via her slave, Eliza Hopewell, who carried the messages in a hollowed-out watchcase.

In scoring her coup at Front Royal, Belle Boyd showed considerable pluck. One evening in mid-May, as General James Shields and his staff conferred in the parlor of the local hotel, Belle hid upstairs, eavesdropping through a knothole in the floor. She learned that Shields had been ordered east, a move that would sap the Federal strength in Front Royal. That night Belle rode through Federal lines, using false papers to bluff her way past the sentries, and reported the news to Colonel Turner Ashby, who was scouting for the Confederates. She then returned to town.

When the Confederates advanced on Front Royal on May 23, Belle braved the fire of Federal skirmishers; as bullets tore holes in her skirt, she ran to greet Jackson's men. She urged an officer to inform Jackson that "the Yankee force is very small. Tell him to charge right down and he will catch them all."

Jackson did so, speedily and successfully. That evening he penned a note of gratitude to Belle Boyd: "I thank you, for myself and for the army, for the immense service that you have rendered your country to-day."

has arrived here." That was the signal for McDowell to put his 40,000 men in motion for the assault on Richmond.

The first step in Jackson's effort to thwart the grand Federal plan was simplicity itself: He meant to swallow the small Federal force at Front Royal in one gulp, meanwhile cutting off its communications with Banks at Strasburg. To that end, Ashby and a contingent of troopers forded the South Fork of the Shenandoah River at sunrise on May 23 and rode to the northwest.

Their mission was to capture a depot and rail trestle at Buckton, thereby severing the link between Banks at Strasburg and his Front Royal outpost. Ashby found the two enemy infantry companies mostly holed up in the depot, a stout brick building that the Federals had converted into a redoubt. Ashby's troopers stormed the structure. They were repulsed by Federals firing through improvised gun ports. Finally a Confederate squad fought its way into the makeshift fortress, and after a few minutes of fighting from room to room a Confederate officer triumphantly emerged with a U.S. flag on his arm. The stronghold taken, Ashby put the depot to the torch, cut telegraph wires, tore up track and headed off to join Jackson at Front Royal.

Jackson's foot soldiers, meanwhile, were struggling toward Front Royal with Ewell and his troops bringing up the rear; despite their new marching discipline, scores of men fell from the ranks with leg and stomach cramps or collapsed from the heat of the blazing day.

As the road they were taking neared Front Royal, it ran alongside the South Fork on a flood plain that could be swept by Federal guns. Seeking higher and safer ground from which he might also swoop down and surprise the enemy garrison, Jackson led his column onto a detour — a crude path with the memorable name of Gooney Manor Road.

At the crest of a 500-foot rise, Jackson paused to survey the scene below. The little town of Front Royal was about a mile to the north. Two miles beyond, the South and North Forks of the Shenandoah River joined for the northerly run to the Potomac at Harpers Ferry. The enemy's tents were pitched near the confluence, on the east bank of the South Fork — the same side from which Jackson now gazed down upon them. To escape from Jackson's clutches, Colonel Kenly and his troops would first have to cross at least one of the two bridges spanning the South Fork, then traverse the single bridge across the North Fork. The complete success of Jackson's onslaught would thus depend on the outcome of a race for the bridges.

Deploying his forces for the attack, Jackson assigned the center of his line to Roberdeau Wheat's ferocious Tigers and to the 1st Maryland (C.S.A.) Regiment — bitter border-state enemy of Kenly's 1st Maryland (U.S.). As it happened, the Confederate Marylanders had recently come close to mutiny because the applications of many men to transfer to the cavalry had been rejected. Indeed, that morning their commander, Colonel Bradley Johnson, had found it necessary to berate his sulking troops.

"Go home," Johnson had cried. "Boast of it when you meet your fathers and mothers, brothers and sisters and sweethearts. Tell them that it was you who, when brought face to face with the enemy, proved yourselves to be cowards."

The armies of Generals Jackson and Ewell swarm over Colonel John Kenly's outnumbered Federals at Front Royal on May 23, 1862. A few Federal soldiers are withdrawing across one of the bridges spanning the South Fork of the Shenandoah River (*background*) — a retreat that soon became a rout.

The challenge to their courage had galvanized the Maryland men, and now they were eager to fight.

As Jackson's skirmishers silently moved forward, they were spotted by a single Federal picket, who fired a futile shot and took to his heels. It was about 2 p.m., and the Battle of Front Royal had begun.

In Front Royal, the townspeople joyfully anticipated their deliverance from enemy hands. Nineteen-year-old Lucy Buck wrote in her diary of hearing "the quick, sharp report of a rifle, and another and another in rapid succession. Going to the door we saw Yankees scampering over the meadow below our house and were at a loss to account for such evident excitement on their part.

"Presently Miss B. White rushed in with purple face and dishevelled hair crying, 'Oh, my God! The Hill above the town is black with our boys.' "

Lucy Buck's own first glimpse of the attacking force was of "a grey figure upon horseback seemingly in command. Seeing was believing, and I could only sink on my knees with my face in my hands and sob for joy."

Front Royal itself was cleared of Federals quickly, but Kenly and his vastly outnumbered force were making a gallant stand on a hill north of town. Colonel Stapleton Crutchfield, who had recently been appointed Jackson's artillery commander, ordered Ewell's guns up to the front. Crutchfield, however, had failed to familiarize himself with Ewell's ordnance — and, to his great chagrin, he now learned that it consisted mostly of light, smoothbore pieces that were easily outranged by the enemy's heavier, rifled cannon.

There seemed nothing for it but to hurl the

infantry against the hill. With the 1st Maryland assigned to assail the Federal center and with Taylor's Louisiana Brigade moving to the enemy's left flank, the men surged ahead. Just then, however, Kenly saw Confederate cavalry on the opposite side of the river moving toward the bridges — his only means of escape.

Without a moment to lose, Kenly ordered his men to abandon their hill and to run for the bridges. Racing for survival, they pounded first across the South Fork spans and then the wooden North Fork structure, which they set afire behind them.

Taylor's brigade, with Taylor and Jackson in the forefront, came hard after the fleeing Federals, arriving at the burning bridge ahead of the Confederate cavalry. With a curt nod, Jackson ordered Taylor across before the bridge collapsed.

"It was rather a near thing," Taylor wrote. "My horse and clothing were scorched, and many men burned their hands severely while throwing brands into the river. Just as I emerged from flames and smoke, Jackson was by my side. How he got there was a mystery, as the bridge was thronged with my men going at full speed, but smoke and fire had decidedly freshened up his costume."

In the distance but well within artillery range was Kenly's column of fleeing Federals, heading toward Winchester. "Oh," cried Jackson, "what an opportunity for artillery! Oh, that my guns were here!" And then he commanded a staff officer to go to the rear and "order up every rifled gun and every brigade in the army."

He was now frustrated by faulty communications. An hour or so earlier, just after he had launched his initial assault against Front Royal, Jackson had sent back word for the

At the Battle of Front Royal, Colonel Bradley T. Johnson (*left*), commander of the Confederate 1st Maryland Regiment, led his men against those of Colonel John Kenly (*inset*), commander of the U.S. Army's 1st Maryland Regiment. The Confederates won the day and climaxed their victory by seizing the Federals' flag (*right*). "The real 1st Maryland had whipped the bogus," exulted Confederate troops.

rest of his men and most of his guns to take the direct route into town rather than the more circuitous Gooney Manor Road.

But Ashby, who was responsible for providing couriers, had on that day assigned one of his least disciplined companies to the task — and the youth entrusted with Jackson's message had fled upon hearing the sounds of battle. As a result, the guns so urgently needed by Jackson at this moment of splendid opportunity were still laboring along Gooney Manor Road.

Yet even as his hopes seemed to be sinking, Jackson caught sight of the cavalry — about 250 troopers under Lieutenant Colo-

nel Thomas Flournoy. Instead of going with Ashby to Buckton, Flournoy had been detached to cut telegraph wires just to the west of Front Royal, and now he and his men were returning.

At Jackson's command, the cavalry contingent rushed in headlong pursuit of the Federals, forcing Kenly's infantry to halt and deploy for a stand at Cedarville, approximately three miles north of Front Royal on the road to Winchester.

His infantry still far behind, Jackson ordered Flournoy to charge the enemy line — 250 troopers against more than three times as many infantry. To the clarion of bugles the Confederate troopers flung themselves against the center of the Federal line.

The line broke. When some of the Federals began to re-form, Flournoy charged again, and this time the enemy was shattered beyond salvation. Jackson later exclaimed that he had never seen so gallant a charge.

In the fighting at Front Royal and Cedarville, the Federals took a beating. Kenly, who had been badly wounded, lost 904 men, of whom 750 were captured. Jackson's casualties numbered only 35.

That night, near Cedarville, Jackson took a seat at Richard Taylor's campfire. Although Taylor "fancied he looked at me kindly," Jackson said scarcely a word. Instead, Taylor recalled, "for hours he sat silent and motionless, with eyes fixed upon the fire, and he remained throughout the night."

Poor Banks. His dreams of victory were fading fast.

The 23rd of May had begun promisingly enough. The Valley countryside around Strasburg was at its springtime best. "Trees of richest verdure were bathed in the morning sun," wrote a Federal officer, "and fields sparkled with dew-drops shining amidst luxuriant grasses."

Banks and his men relaxed, basking in a false sense of security. As George Gordon recalled: "A general languor was manifested in the drowsy way in which the sentinels dawdled along their posts, or in the aimless sleepy air in which the troops addressed themselves."

That tranquillity was obliterated at about 4 p.m. by the arrival of a courier bearing news that the Federal garrison at Front Royal was under attack. Hardly were the words out of his mouth than another messenger stormed into town on a sweat-lathered horse. He carried even worse tidings: Front Royal itself had fallen and the enemy was now crossing the burning North Fork bridge.

In his ignorance, Banks insisted that the events taking place to the east at Front Royal were no more than a diversion and that the real threat to his Strasburg position lay in an attack from the south. That view was reinforced at dusk, when a small band of Confederate cavalry — which had been sent toward Strasburg with the specific purpose of distracting Banks — audaciously seized a weakly defended hill outside town. Darkness concealed the actual size of the attacking force — and Banks spent the night in the misapprehension that he was confronted by an entire Confederate division.

Other Federal officers knew better, and tried to convince Banks that the real threat lay elsewhere. Early in the evening Colonel Gordon went to the commanding general's tent to argue that if Banks did not immediately withdraw to Winchester he would almost certainly be cut off from that base by the Confederates now threatening his flank at Front Royal.

But Banks, still bothered by thoughts of Confederates on the nearby hill, responded again and again: "I must develop the force of the enemy." Recalled Gordon: "No argument could suppress this monotonous utterance. Banks seemed brooding over thoughts he did not reveal; he was spiritless and dejected."

Still pressing his pleas, Gordon finally kindled a spark in Banks. "By God, sir," Banks said, angrily arising from his chair, "I will not retreat." Then he added: "We have more to fear from the opinions of our friends than the bayonets of our enemies."

Suddenly it dawned on Gordon: The Bobbin Boy of Waltham was worried about the public response to a retreat. Gordon was convinced that Banks was placing political considerations ahead of military ones. "This, sir," said Gordon, "is not a military ground for occupying a false position." Then he stalked from the tent.

But as the night wore on, the seriousness of his plight began to sink in on Banks. At about 3 a.m. he ordered that his sick and wounded be sent to Winchester. At midmorning of May 24, he finally put his infantry on the road, grandiloquently explaining to Washington that he had determined "to enter the lists with the enemy in a race or a battle (as he should choose) for the possession of Winchester."

During his campfire vigil, Jackson pondered the Front Royal-Strasburg-Winchester road system — the key to intercepting Banks's forces. From Front Royal to Winchester a road ran northwest 20 miles; from Strasburg to Winchester the Valley Turnpike led 18 miles northeast; running west to east was the 10-mile-long road from Strasburg to Front Royal.

Jackson could see that the Union commander had several options. One of them — crossing the Alleghenies to join Frémont on the South Fork of the South Branch of the Potomac — could safely be ruled out; on its east-west line of march, the Federal column would be exposed to a flank attack from the south. A second choice seemed just as unlikely: Even in his most sanguine moments, Jackson could hardly imagine Banks being foolish enough to fight it out from his isolated location at Strasburg.

That left two realistic possibilities. The Federal troops could either make a dash for Winchester, or if Jackson abandoned Front Royal in his own rush for Winchester, Banks might slip his troops behind the Confederates, pass through Front Royal and run for refuge across the Blue Ridge.

Jackson devised a plan. It hinged on another road, one running diagonally from the Front Royal-Winchester road at Cedarville to the Valley pike at Middletown, five miles north of Strasburg. If Banks moved toward Winchester, Jackson could slice across and strike the marching column while it was passing through Middletown. However, until Jackson received news of such a Federal movement, the bulk of his army would have to remain near enough to Front Royal to cut off Banks in case he tried to escape across the Blue Ridge.

Orders were issued accordingly. Ashby's scouts would keep an eye on the Strasburg-Front Royal Road. Two regiments of Ewell's cavalry under Brigadier General George H. Steuart were sent cross-country toward Newtown, 4 miles north of Middletown, to scout for the enemy vanguard moving along the pike. Ewell was to take the bulk of his forces toward Winchester, but halt them before they got too far out of reach.

The rest of the army, including Taylor's troops, would come up to Cedarville and await further developments. Once they had closed ranks, most of the men fell out and lazed along the roadside near Cedarville. At 11 a.m. a courier burst upon the somnolent scene with the word so eagerly anticipated by Jackson. The message was from Steuart, whose troopers had arrived at Newtown — where they beheld the Valley pike choked with Federal supply wagons making haste for Winchester.

No more time could be lost. Ashby, now freed from watching the Strasburg-Front Royal road, took the lead on the crossroad to Middletown. With him went Colonel Robert P. Chew's horse artillery and two rifled guns of the Rockbridge Artillery, escorted by the Louisiana Tigers battalion. Behind them, driving hard, came the rest of Taylor's brigade and the regiments of the Valley army. The remainder of Ewell's command stayed on the Cedarville-Winchester road, poised either to act as a reserve at Middletown or to march on Winchester later.

Despite Jackson's sense of urgency, the drive to Middletown was slow, for his men had to contend with Federal troopers. Five companies of the 1st Maine Cavalry and two companies of the 1st Vermont Cavalry forced the Confederates to stop frequently and fight. Finally, just before 3 p.m., Jackson's men came upon a rise overlooking Middletown, and feasted their eyes on Banks's force in full retreat to Winchester.

Instants later, Jackson's guns roared. "At a half mile range," wrote a Confederate artillerist, "we opened with all of our guns, and as our shells plowed gap after gap through the serried column it caused consternation, confounded and vastly increased the speed of the mixed fugitive mass."

Jackson watched the artillery attack. "The road," he wrote later, "was literally obstructed with the mingled and confused mass of struggling and dying horses and riders." Henry Kyd Douglas recorded that he would never forget "the bleeding pile, a roaring, shrieking, struggling mass of men and horses, crushed, wounded and dying. It was a sickening sight, the worst I had ever seen."

Then the Tigers pounced, slashing and pillaging. "The gentle Tigers," wrote Rich-ard Taylor ironically, "were looting right merrily, diving in and out of wagons with the activity of rabbits in a warren; but this occupation was abandoned on my approach, and in a moment they were in line, looking as solemn and virtuous as deacons at a funeral."

Suddenly, at about 4 p.m., the booming of cannons came from the south, where Federal artillery and infantry appeared to have taken a strong position just west of the turnpike. While Taylor wheeled to meet their threat,

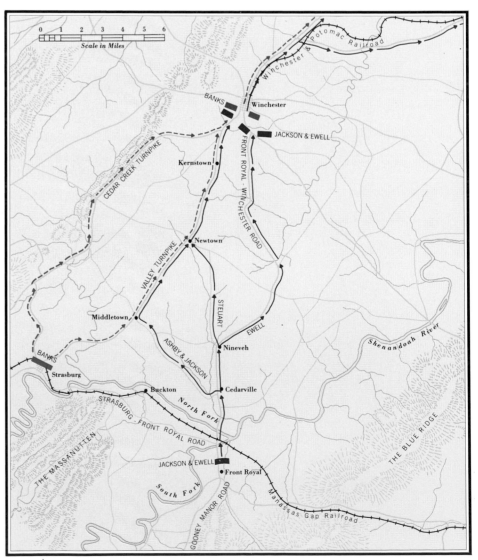

Stonewall Jackson seized Front Royal on May 23, prompting Nathaniel Banks's main force at Strasburg to withdraw northward on the Valley Turnpike toward Winchester. Jackson, striking from Cedarville, severed the tail of the retreating Federal column at Middletown while Richard Ewell pushed on to Winchester. On May 25, Jackson's forces joined Ewell's to defeat Banks in a pitched battle south of the town; the Federals fell back toward the Potomac with Jackson in pursuit.

Jackson ordered the artillery and Ashby's cavalrymen to pursue and punish the bluecoats still fleeing north.

Taylor's deployment took time, and before it was completed the Federals who confronted him had withdrawn. Not until then did Jackson realize that he had been distracted by a rear guard making a valiant stand. The main body of Banks's army had already passed through Middletown and was even now escaping the trap that Jackson had

In a daring raid on occupied Newtown, Confederate cavalrymen waylay surprised Federal soldiers on a hotel porch. The Northern paper that published this illustration called the raid an atrocity, claiming that the hotel was a Federal hospital.

so laboriously laid. The general now sent word to Ewell, north of Cedarville, to proceed to Winchester and deploy for an attack south of the town.

Then Jackson quickly sent his foot soldiers on a chase down the Valley pike. They caught up with the Confederate cavalry and artillery just beyond Newtown. There artillery commander Crutchfield seethed in a towering fury. Far from pressing the pursuit, Ashby's troopers had stopped to plunder the wagons abandoned along the turnpike. Having defied Crutchfield's shouted curses and threats, many of the cavalrymen were by now drunk on whiskey from Federal kegs. "Unable to force or persuade them to abandon this disgraceful employment," Crutchfield wrote later, "I returned to Newtown, and after consulting Colonel Ashby we concluded it would be imprudent to push the pursuit further."

The foot soldiers were allowed no respite. Push on, came the command from Jackson, and the men moved into the night. Impeded by abandoned Federal wagons, beset by ambushes, groping in the darkness, they measured their progress by mere yards.

"Step by step we moved along, halting for five minutes; then a few steps and halt again," recalled one Confederate. Wrote another: "Moving at a snail's pace and falling asleep at the halts and being suddenly wakened up when motion was resumed, we fairly staggered on, worn almost to exhaustion by the weariness of such a march."

Sometime after 1 a.m., Colonel Sam Fulkerson, commander of the 37th Virginia, approached Jackson with a request. "General," he said, "if I may be permitted to make a suggestion, I think the troops had better be rested for an hour or so; my men are falling

Music to Fight by

"I wish my darling could be with me now," General Stonewall Jackson wrote to his wife, Anna, in 1861, "and enjoy the sweet music of the brass band of the Fifth Regiment. It is an excellent band."

The musicians of the 5th Virginia Infantry, named the Stonewall Brigade Band by special order of their general, provided Jackson's army with much more than sweet music. In addition to their instruments, the bandsmen carried late-model Austrian rifles, and when battle was joined they fought side by side with their regiment. On occasion they doubled as couriers and litter-bearers, and were sometimes called upon to assist surgeons. For these duties the men drew $12 a month, a dollar more than a private's pay; the drum major and chief musician each received $21 a month.

The band's role in the fighting could be costly. When Jackson's troops recaptured Winchester on May 25, 1862, the musicians insisted on leading the riflemen into town. Cornets and saxhorns blaring, they paraded straight into the fire of Federal snipers, and two of the men were severely wounded.

During peaceful interludes the Stonewall Brigade Band gave concerts in towns near battle sites in order to spur enlistments and raise relief funds for soldiers' families. On picket duty along the Rappahannock one winter, the musicians exchanged nightly serenades with a Federal band encamped on the opposite bank. After the Yankees played "Home Sweet Home" and "The Star Spangled Banner," the Confederates responded with their own spirited renditions of "The Bonnie Blue Flag" and "Dixie."

The band continued to perform as a unit long after the Stonewall Brigade itself was dissolved. Seven of the 14 bandsmen surrendered together at Appomattox; of the band's instruments, only two cracked drums and nine battered silver horns survived the War.

The Stonewall Brigade Band drew eight of its members from the Staunton Mountain Sax Horn Band (above), formed in 1845 by Augustus J. Turner (top row). The War took a heavy toll on Jackson's bandsmen: One musician died in battle, six were wounded and two were taken prisoner.

by the roadside from fatigue and loss of sleep. Unless they are rested, I shall be able to present but a thin line tomorrow."

"Colonel," replied Jackson, "I yield to no man in sympathy for the gallant men under my command; but I am obliged to sweat them tonight, that I may save their blood tomorrow. The line of hills southwest of Winchester must not be occupied by the enemy's artillery. My own must be there and in position by daylight."

And then, in sudden pity: "You shall, however, have two hours rest."

The men slept where they fell.

Jackson himself stood watch, a lone wakeful figure among the slumbering soldiers. At about 4 a.m. he ordered the men aroused, and they soon filed silently into an early-morning fog that hung heavy over the approaches to Winchester. It was the 25th of May — another Sunday on which Stonewall Jackson would fight.

Winchester, on its south and southwest, was guarded by the hills that had worried Jackson during the previous night's march. Now, his scouts provided the pleasing news that the nearest ridge was only weakly held by enemy skirmishers. As it turned out, Banks had felt reasonably secure upon his arrival in Winchester the previous evening; after deploying his troops for a defense, he had taken a warm bath and gone to bed. Probably recalling the problems caused by inadequate reconnaissance at Kernstown, Jackson rode forward to look for himself. He was quickly satisfied that the Federals had failed to occupy the line of hills in strength.

Up came the Stonewall Brigade's commander, Charles Winder, crisp and starched as always. Jackson pointed to a ridge commanding the turnpike and issued a curt order: "You must occupy that hill."

As Winder prepared to move, Jackson heard firing across the Valley pike on his right. The sound meant that Richard Ewell was in place. Following Jackson's orders, Ewell had marched down the Front Royal-Winchester road late the previous afternoon and had deployed south of Winchester at nightfall.

Winder's Stonewall Brigade made it up their assigned hill quickly and with little opposition. But when the men gained the crest of the hill, they were almost immediately pinned down by a storm of artillery and small arms fire pouring in from a second ridge on the southwest corner of Winchester. That strongly held ridge anchored the right of Banks's line, which stretched more than a half mile southeast across the turnpike.

Winder requested help from Jackson, who replied: "I will send you up Taylor."

Jackson found the Louisianian at the head of his brigade, already moving up from his position in reserve. Pointing to the troublesome hill that keyed the extreme right flank of the Federal line, Jackson said simply: "You must carry it."

As Taylor moved forward, meaning to skirt the hill and take it in a flanking attack, he found Jackson again beside him. Just then, the brigade came under galling artillery fire from the hill. The men flinched — and Taylor was furious. "What the hell are you dodging for?" he shouted. "If there is any more of it, you will be halted under this fire for an hour."

Jackson touched Taylor's shoulder and glanced at him with what Taylor called reproachful surprise. "I am afraid," Jackson said quietly, "you are a wicked fellow."

Then he rode away to watch the battle.

The Louisianians, their pelican banners flapping, started forward, slowly at first and then with a surge. The rest of the army thrilled at the sight. "That charge of Taylor's was the grandest I saw during the war," recalled a Confederate private. Wrote Jackson's chief of staff, the Reverend Major Dabney: "The enemy poured grape and musketry into Taylor's line as soon as it came in sight. Gen. Taylor rode in front of his brigade, drawn sword in hand, occasionally turning his horse, at other times merely turning in his saddle to see that his line was up. They marched up the hill in perfect order, not firing a shot! About half-way to the Yankees in a loud and commanding voice that I am sure the Yankees heard, he gave the order to charge!"

The Louisiana men, supported by the hard-firing Rockbridge Artillery and a battery under the command of Lieutenant William Poague, surged up the hill. Across the pike, Ewell's troops were outflanking the extreme left of the Federal line. Everywhere the Confederates surged forward. The Federal defenses bent, then broke under the weight of the attack, and the blueclad soldiers fled, racing rearward through the streets of Winchester.

Jackson was wild with excitement. "The battle's won!" he cried. "Very good! Now let's holler!" Sweeping off his hat, the commanding general rode after the fleeing Federals, cheering and whooping as loudly as any of the teen-age boys who followed him.

When an officer protested at Jackson's exposed position, the general commanded: "Go back and tell the whole army to press forward to the Potomac!"

The Confederate pursuit was enthusiastic but badly muddled — partly because Ashby, contrary to orders, had gone off in chase of a Federal detachment. Now, when his troopers were most urgently needed, the cavalry was wandering about the countryside. "Never was there such a chance for cavalry," shouted Jackson as the enemy columns hurried northward beyond his clutches. "Oh, that my cavalry was in place!"

Banks, who had lost about 3,500 men — or nearly 35 per cent of his total command — at Front Royal and Winchester, did his best to bring order to the rout. "Stop, men!" he cried to some Wisconsin troops. "Don't you love your country?" Replied one of the men: "Yes, by God, and I'm trying to get back to it just as fast as I can!"

During the 14 hours following Jackson's assault on Winchester, the Federal force that had opposed him covered no fewer than 35 miles. When the beaten and exhausted Yankees crossed the Potomac into Williamsport, Maryland, they seemed to breathe a huge collective sigh of relief. Said Banks of the moment when his defeated troops stood at last on Union ground: "There were never more grateful hearts."

Despite the failure of his pursuit, Jackson had accomplished a major strategic goal. Upon hearing of the Confederate capture of Front Royal — and even before Jackson's victory at Winchester — the President of the United States had wired General George McClellan near Richmond: "In consequence of General Banks's critical position I have been compelled to suspend General McDowell's movements to join you." The great Federal movement on the Confederate capital had been stymied by the Valley army.

A Fortress City on the Potomac

"Before the war the city was as drowsy and as grass-grown as any old New England town," journalist Noah Brooks recalled of Washington, D.C. "The war changed all that in a very few weeks."

Indeed, by the spring of 1862, when Stonewall Jackson's Confederate army threatened Washington from the Shenandoah Valley, the Federal capital fairly bristled with defenses. "Long lines of army wagons and artillery were con-tinually rumbling through the streets," Brooks reported. At the same time construction crews were erecting a cordon of fieldworks that would turn Washington into the most heavily fortified place in the United States.

The architect of this transformation was a 47-year-old engineer, Brigadier General John G. Barnard, whom Mc-Clellan had appointed to bolster the city's defenses after the Federal dis-

The 1st Connecticut Heavy Artillery Regiment drills at a fort on the Arlington heights, which command Washington from the Virginia side of the Potomac River.

aster at Bull Run. Under Barnard's supervision, 3,000 soldiers and civilian laborers constructed dozens of enclosed field forts and batteries occupying every prominent point around the city at intervals of 800 to 1,000 yards.

The forts were relatively simple structures made of wood and earth. Workers dug a ditch around the planned perimeter and piled the dirt inside to form an embankment called a rampart.

Heavy guns were positioned on the ramparts on wooden platforms. Then living quarters, powder magazines, guardhouses and bombproofs were erected inside the enclosure.

Between the forts, Barnard's crews built lunettes — crescent-shaped earthen emplacements for fieldpieces — that commanded the approaches to the city. And the whole system was connected by 20 miles of trenches for riflemen.

The massive construction project was carried out with picks and shovels in what a soldier from the 79th New York Regiment called "the hardest kind of manual labor." But when completed and fully garrisoned by 25,000 infantry and 9,000 artillerymen, General Barnard's interlocking network of fortified positions was truly formidable. The once peaceful capital on the Potomac had become a fortress city.

Federal infantrymen guard Chain Bridge, the northernmost of three bridges that spanned the Potomac between Washington and Virginia during the War.

Artillerymen at Battery Martin Scott
(*inset*) stand to their guns on the
heights overlooking the Virginia
approaches to Chain Bridge. This
battery, named for an officer killed
during the Mexican War, was one
of the first heavy gun emplacements
to be built by the Federals.

Artillerymen at Fort Totten, north of Washington, assemble outside an earthwork bombproof large enough to shelter the entire garrison.

On the Virginia side of the Potomac, civilian laborers *(inset)* dig a trench around the stockade guarding the machine shop and yards of the Orange & Alexandria Railroad. "Spades were trumps," quipped a New Yorker who witnessed the work, "and every man held a full hand."

A log blockhouse, whose two canted levels provided clear fields of fire in all directions, protects an approach to a bridge over Hunting Creek in Alexandria.

Federal troops at Fort Slemmer, on the outskirts of the capital, march through a sally port and past a defensive barrier of cut trees known as an abatis.

The Victorious Retreat

"In advance, his trains were left far behind. In retreat, he would fight for a wheelbarrow."

BRIGADIER GENERAL RICHARD TAYLOR, THE LOUISIANA BRIGADE, SPEAKING OF JACKSON

5 The distressing word that Banks had been routed at Winchester threw a scare into official Washington, giving rise to panicky second thoughts about the security of the capital. In particular, the excitable Stanton reacted with what one of his own friends later described as "the flurry of a girl who meets a cow in the street."

To the governors of 13 Northern states, Stanton sent a frantic telegram: "Intelligence from various quarters leaves no doubt that the enemy in great force are advancing on Washington. You will please organize and forward immediately all the volunteer and militia force in your state." To speed the gathering of reinforcements for Washington, Stanton assumed operating control of all Northern railroads.

Lincoln, too, was affected. He wired McClellan outside Richmond, demanding that he either attack the Confederate capital or return to defend Washington. Said Lincoln: "Let me hear from you instantly."

McClellan's official reply was straightforward enough: "Telegram received. Independently of it, the time is very near when I shall attack Richmond." But in a letter written that day to his wife, he was contemptuous of the President. Lincoln, he said, was "terribly scared. Heaven help a country governed by such counsels." That night, adding to the letter after receiving another message from Lincoln, the general seemed to be gloating over the discomfiture of his civilian superiors. "A scare will do them good," he noted, "and may bring them to their senses."

However apprehensive Lincoln may have been, he had far from lost his senses. In fact, the President had been making plans on his own to end the threat to Washington from the Shenandoah Valley. When Lincoln got the alarming news of Stonewall Jackson's strike against Front Royal, he straightaway began devising a strategy that would involve three separate Federal commands.

Lincoln believed that Jackson's incursion was more than merely a raid. The President thought that the Confederates would continue their northward thrust through Winchester and probably to the Potomac. To make certain that Jackson did not cross the Potomac and turn southeast for an advance on Washington, the President would heavily reinforce the hapless Banks. Then, while Jackson snapped and snarled on the south side of the Potomac, Lincoln would lay a trap behind him — and spring it shut.

A ready tool for that task was John C. Frémont, presently awaiting a call to action at Franklin, in the Alleghenies only 30 miles northwest of Harrisonburg. A rapid march by Frémont to Harrisonburg would place him 80 miles to Jackson's rear, squarely athwart the Confederate supply line and in a position to block any attempt by the Valley army to escape southward along the turnpike. Thus the President ordered Frémont to march to Harrisonburg "and operate against the enemy in such a way as to relieve Banks." Lincoln added: "This move-

This so-called bullet-proof vest was discarded by its owner during Jackson's Valley Campaign. The heavy and cumbersome iron jackets were sold to gullible recruits on both sides in the early days of the War; they all but immobilized the wearer and were seldom used in battle.

ment must be made immediately. Put the utmost speed into it. Do not lose a minute."

So much for Frémont — or so Lincoln thought. Next, having suspended McDowell's march on Richmond, Lincoln ordered McDowell to prepare to move part of his force to the Valley at Front Royal, where it would remain poised along the route of Jackson's retreat. When and if Jackson withdrew to the south, Banks would harry his rear. At the same time, McDowell's detachment at Front Royal would be ready to attack and pursue, pounding the Valley army against Frémont's position at Harrisonburg. Thus McDowell and Banks would be the Federal hammers, and Frémont the anvil.

The President's plan was no less than a move to destroy the Valley army. It was also a highly complex scheme that depended for its success on close coordination and crisp execution. By this point in the War, Abraham Lincoln was sorely aware of his generals' almost infinite capacity for failing to follow his instructions. Furthermore, McDowell had expressed bitter disappointment that his advance on Richmond had again been delayed. Just to make sure nothing went wrong, the President decided to send a personal representative to see that McDowell complied with his instructions. Lincoln's choice was the Treasury Secretary, Salmon P. Chase.

Shortly after Chase arrived at McDowell's headquarters on Sunday, May 25, he received a telegram from Lincoln with an implicit suggestion as to how he might encourage the disappointed general. "It will be a very valuable and very honorable service for General McDowell to cut them off," the President wrote. "I hope he will put all possible energy and speed into the effort." Replied Chase: "General McDowell appreciates, as you do, the importance of the service he is called on to perform. All possible exertion is being made by him and the officers under him to expedite the movement."

By nightfall, one of McDowell's divisions commanded by Brigadier General Shields, having just arrived from the Valley to join the advance on Richmond, was on its way back to the Shenandoah. Banks had gained safety on the Maryland side of the Potomac and was regrouping his battered forces. All in all, Lincoln's plan seemed to be progressing nicely. The President, however, had reckoned without John C. Frémont's proclivity for waywardness.

For his explorations in the West, Frémont had won fame, fortune and a nickname — the Pathfinder. He married the daughter of Missouri's powerful Senator Thomas Hart Benton; he was elected to the U.S. Senate from California; and in 1856 he became the first presidential nominee of the fledgling Republican Party.

Frémont, possessing such sterling political credentials, was appointed a major general by Lincoln in 1861, and his self-esteem seems to have risen to new heights. Placed in command of the sprawling Western Department, with headquarters in St. Louis, he soon earned a reputation, as a Federal soldier put it, for being a "spread-eagle, show-off, horn-tooting general."

Ensconced in an imposing mansion, he surrounded himself with popinjay aides from foreign countries, men given to strutting about in the full-dress uniforms of their former European commands. Frémont also risked alienating border-state loyalties by issuing — without a word to the President —

his own emancipation proclamation. And, worst of all, he displayed a notable disinclination for hard fighting.

Lincoln's patience finally ran out, and he removed Frémont from his post in the West; later, however, under heavy political pressure, the President appointed him to command in the remote Alleghenies, where presumably he could do little harm. Yet even there, Frémont came up with a grandiose plan: Given reinforcements, he would first capture Staunton, which would then be used as a base for a triumphant march on Knoxville, Tennessee, 300 miles to the southwest. Jackson's victory at McDowell, just west of Staunton, put an end to Frémont's dream, and the Federal general had since spent most of his time at his Franklin headquarters complaining about his supply situation.

And now, with an opportunity to make a real contribution by carrying out Lincoln's orders, Frémont erred again. Instead of marching to Harrisonburg to assume a blocking position as commanded, Frémont was heading toward Strasburg to cut off Jackson—thereby increasing his marching distance by at least 40 miles. On May 27, Lincoln learned that Frémont was at Moorefield, 40 miles north of Franklin, and moving farther in the wrong direction. The President was livid: "I see that you are at Moorefield," Lincoln wired. "You were expressly ordered to march to Harrisonburg. What does this mean?"

In his reply, sent at 6 a.m. the next day, Frémont was the soul of injured innocence: "In executing any order received I take it for granted that I am to exercise discretion concerning its literal execution, according to circumstances. If I am to understand that literal obedience to orders is required, please say

so. I have no desire to exercise any power which you do not think belongs of necessity to my position in the field."

The damage had been done. Frémont's troops were now much closer to Strasburg than Harrisonburg; to reverse them would simply waste more valuable time. What to do? Lincoln made a decision early that evening, and Secretary Stanton wired: "The President directs you to move upon Jackson by the best route you can."

Now Lincoln's original plan had been turned into a difficult pincers movement, with Frémont attacking from the west and Shields from the east. Everything depended on perfect timing; the two forces had to reach their destinations before Jackson slipped through on a withdrawal up the Valley.

On Monday, May 26, at Winchester, Jackson had declared a day of worship to make up for the one the army had missed while seizing the town. The following night, while Jackson was sleeping, an elderly and exhausted civilian rode up to the general's headquarters bearing dire news. He had seen Shields's column moving toward Front Royal and had ridden more than 12 hours to warn Jackson.

The old man impressed Jackson's staff. "His grey hairs, intelligence, and dignity of manner," recalled Henry Kyd Douglas, "convinced us that he was no sensationalist." Nonetheless, Jackson's aides were reluctant to awaken their commander, and it was not until early morning that the general interviewed the old man. Then, although Jackson was clearly persuaded that strong enemy forces were closing in on him, he ordered his army to move — not southward toward safety but northward, deeper into danger. Jackson had received word from

General Lee urging him to threaten the line of the Potomac, and he meant to do just that.

On May 29 and the morning of May 30, therefore, while Jackson and most of the Valley army camped near Charles Town, Charles Winder and his Stonewall Brigade demonstrated against Harpers Ferry. Even on the afternoon of May 30, when Ashby's scouts brought word from the Blue Ridge that Shields was less than a day's march from Front Royal, Jackson appeared unperturbed. While he napped under a tree, his young staff members again shook their heads at their chief's peculiar ways. Muttered one of the more erudite aides: "*Quem deus vult perdere, prius dementat*" — those whom the gods would destroy, they first make mad.

The general awakened to find his old friend Alexander Boteler, the U.S. Congressman now commissioned as a colonel, drawing his likeness. Examining the sketch, Jackson mused on his own lack of artistic skills. "My hardest tasks at West Point," he said, "were the drawing lessons, and I never could do anything in that line to satisfy myself, or indeed, anyone else."

Then, in an abrupt change of mood, he was all business. He told Boteler to leave at once for Richmond to seek reinforcements. If enough were available, Jackson said, a move "may be made beyond the Potomac, which will soon raise the siege of Richmond and transfer this campaign from the banks of the Potomac to those of the Susquehanna."

But Jackson doubted the success of Boteler's mission: Hardly had the emissary left when the general ordered his army to start south, leaving behind only the Stonewall Brigade to make a final feint against Harpers Ferry. Then, late on May 30, Jackson himself departed Charles Town for Winchester.

As his train rumbled through the rainy night, Jackson fell asleep — only to be awakened by a Confederate horseman who had intercepted the train to give him a message. Silently, Jackson read the courier's message, tore it up and went back to sleep — even though he had just been informed that Shields had captured Front Royal and was now on the flank of the Confederate retreat.

Arriving in Winchester, Jackson summoned into his grim presence a shamefaced Confederate officer: He was Colonel Zephaniah T. Conner, who had abandoned command of his small detachment at Front Royal at the enemy's approach. A 60-year-old captain had taken charge and marched the men in good order to Winchester.

"Colonel," asked Jackson, "how many men did you have killed?"

"None."

"How many wounded?"

"None."

"Do you call that much of a fight?" growled Jackson — placing Conner under arrest.

That night Jackson awakened his mapmaker, Jedediah Hotchkiss, and instructed him to hasten toward Harpers Ferry to fetch Winder and the Stonewall Brigade. According to Hotchkiss' diary, Jackson "feared that the converging columns of Frémont, Shields, McDowell and Banks might compel him to go out and fight one of them, but he was in fine spirits."

The same could hardly be said of Abraham Lincoln as he desperately exhorted his generals to close the trap on Jackson.

"It is for you a question of legs," the President had telegraphed McDowell. "Put in all the speed you can. I have told Frémont as much, and directed him to drive at them as fast as possible."

From Frémont, however, came disquiet-

Ill-equipped and ill-led, Federal soldiers under the command of General John C. Frémont march up the Valley in pursuit of Jackson after crossing the Allegheny Mountains. Frémont had left behind baggage and provisions; many of the men were shoeless; and the army, reported an emissary from President Lincoln, was generally "in a wretched condition."

ing reports. On May 29 he had told Washington that his scouts estimated enemy strength at 60,000 men. Nonsense, replied Lincoln: Jackson's army could number no more than 20,000 and was probably closer to 15,000. "Where is your force?" Lincoln impatiently asked. "It ought this minute to be near Strasburg. Answer at once."

The reply came the next day and was even more discouraging. Complaining about the hardships of his march, Frémont said that he could not possibly promise to be at Strasburg before 5 p.m. on May 31 — more than a day after Shields would arrive at Front Royal.

To make matters worse, Banks claimed his command was still too shaken from its recent experiences to harry Jackson's withdrawal; as it turned out, Banks would remain on the far side of the Potomac until June 10. And Shields, having seized Front Royal, stayed there while waiting for another of McDowell's divisions, under Major General E.O.C. Ord, to come up as reinforcement.

Frémont advanced at a snail's pace. At 8 p.m. on May 31, three hours after his self-ordained deadline for reaching the Valley Turnpike, a message from Frémont arrived in Washington from Wardensville, 15 miles west of Strasburg. "Roads heavy and weather terrible," it said. "Heavy storm of rain most of yesterday and all last night." Then Frémont added with a note of confidence: "The army is pushing forward and I intend to carry out operations proposed."

Meanwhile, during the day, the President had received the alarming news that Joseph Johnston, taking advantage of McDowell's absence, had attacked McClellan just east of Richmond. The confused and bloody battle, called Fair Oaks by the Federals and Seven Pines by the Confederates, lasted two days and ended in a draw; General Johnston was gravely wounded — and was shortly thereafter succeeded in command by Robert E. Lee.

After the crisis at Fair Oaks had passed, Lincoln still had to worry and wait for the answer to another critical question: Could the Union's noose snare Stonewall Jackson?

By 2:30 p.m. on May 31, Jackson's army, less the Stonewall Brigade, had cleared Winchester on the turnpike to Strasburg. First came the supply wagons in a double line eight miles long, heavily laden with captured Union goods and, as the foot soldiers joked, their general's lemons. Then 2,300 Federal prisoners marched under guard. They were followed by Jackson, a scruffy figure on his small horse. Next came the infantry, with Ewell's division at the end of the marching column. Guarding the rear, contingents of Ashby's cavalry extended back toward the Stonewall Brigade on the Potomac.

At dusk, as the column neared Strasburg, Jackson rode ahead to take a look. To the east, there was no sign of Shields. To the west, Frémont had yet to appear. While the wagons continued southward, the army stopped just north of Strasburg, and Jackson issued orders for the next morning. Ewell's command would move from the rear of the infantry to the front, enter Strasburg and then turn off to the west to meet Frémont's expected advance. For as long as Ewell could, he must hold open the Strasburg gate so that the Stonewall Brigade might catch up and pass through.

Ewell was delighted. He had his troops up at dawn. As his skirmishers pushed westward, they came under desultory cannonading from Frémont's advance forces, situated in dense woods about four miles from Stras-

Foreign Gallants in the Union's Cause

When the War broke out, thousands of foreign-born military men descended on Washington to offer their services to the Union cause. "Garibaldians, Hungarians, Poles, officers of Turkish and other contingents surround the State Department," a journalist in the capital observed, "and they infest unsuspecting politicians with illegible testimonials in unknown tongues."

By the spring of 1862, many of the foreigners had won assignments with the Federal forces in the Shenandoah Valley — indeed, the Valley had the largest proportion of foreign-born troops of any theater in the War. Among these men were dozens of Europe's ablest officers. But many others who won important posts were unmitigated charlatans, with inflated or patently false credentials.

The problem of foreign impostors was particularly acute in the army of John C. Frémont. Mesmerized by European military pomp, the impressionable Frémont surrounded himself with foreign aides whose grand titles belied their profound ignorance of military matters. Frémont might have done better to heed the counsel offered in *The New York Times:* "Certainly it is unwise to accept foreign birth and inability to speak the English tongue as prima facie evidence of military education and experience."

General Louis Blenker (*hand on belt*), a German-born division commander under Frémont, is flanked by officers of his division in front of Fairfax Court House, Virginia. Brave but plodding, Blenker emulated "all the pomp of a high commanding general as he had seen it in Europe," recalled the wife of one of his officers. In her words, Blenker resembled "half a Prussian general, half a Turkish pasha."

Gustave Paul Cluseret of France arrived in America in 1862 trumpeting his military exploits in Algeria, the Crimea and Italy. General McClellan sized him up at once as a scoundrel, but he reappeared later as a brigadier general in Frémont's army.

Colonel Frederic D'Utassy (*left*) and Lieutenant Colonel Alex Repetti of the 39th New York, or "Garibaldi Guards," shake hands beneath their regimental banners. The American careers of both officers ended in disgrace: D'Utassy was cashiered for dereliction of duty; Repetti resigned following charges that he had threatened to shoot a gravely ill enlisted man.

An English veteran of half a dozen European campaigns, Sir Percy Wyndham was appointed colonel of the 1st New Jersey Cavalry in 1862. Fearless in battle, he was captured at Harrisonburg, Virginia, by Jackson's rear guard, but later escaped and served well with the Federals until severely wounded in 1863.

Myles Walter Keogh left his native Ireland to fight in the army of Pope Pius IX, and later served as a member of the papal guard at Rome. After joining the Federal Army, he fought with distinction under General Shields in the Valley.

Wladimir Krzyzanowski emigrated to America from Poland in 1846. When the War began he organized the 58th New York Volunteers, a regiment of German and Polish troops that fought in the Valley under Frémont. Krzyzanowski later led brigades at Chancellorsville and Gettysburg, and ended the War as a brigadier general.

burg. While Ewell was surveying the scene, Richard Taylor rode up. For some reason, Taylor was on edge. "Whether from fatigue, loss of sleep, or what, there I was," he recalled, "nervous as a lady, ducking like a mandarin." When Taylor mentioned his skittishness, Ewell laughed, blamed the condition on too much coffee, and advised: "Better give it up."

Growing serious, Ewell told Taylor: "Remain here in charge while I go out to the skirmishers. I can't make out what these people are about, for my skirmish line has stopped them." After riding forward, Ewell returned in a few minutes and admitted: "I am completely puzzled. I have driven everything back to the main body, which is large."

Taylor suggested that he might move his Louisiana Brigade around to the right so as to threaten the Federal flank. Replied Ewell: "Do so. That may stir them up, and I am sick of this fiddling about."

Well rid of his prebattle tremors, Taylor carried out the maneuver, enjoying what he called "a walk-over." Frémont's troops scattered before Taylor's advance. "Sheep would have made as much resistance as we met," Taylor said. It was by now perfectly clear that John C. Frémont represented little menace. For Jackson, only the arrival of the Stonewall Brigade remained for his entire army to escape from Lincoln's trap.

The men of the Stonewall Brigade had gotten off to a belated start. On the morning of May 31, one of Winder's aides had been awakened by somebody stumbling over his tent ropes. It was Jed Hotchkiss. To his vast chagrin, the cartographer had gotten lost on his way to inform Winder that the Stonewall Brigade must hurry southward.

Winder then had to spend several hours collecting the 2nd Virginia Regiment, which had been on the other side of the Shenandoah River, threatening the Federals atop Loudoun Heights outside Harpers Ferry. Cavalry assisted in rounding up the regiment. The foot soldiers recrossed the Shenandoah by holding onto the tails of the troopers' swimming horses. Then, as a soaking rain began to fall, the Stonewall Brigade set off on its march for survival.

At dusk, the brigade trudged through Winchester. At 10 p.m., the column arrived at Newtown, 10 miles from Strasburg and the remainder of Jackson's army. The men were on their last legs. During the day, they had marched at least 28 miles, and the 2nd Virginia had trekked 35. Stragglers were falling out by the hundreds. Despite his reputation as a martinet, Charles Winder knew that his men could go no farther, and he ordered a halt for the night.

The troops were back on the road by sunrise. Their mood was somber. A soldier recalled: "Officers and men were silent as the grave — occupied all with the same gloomy apprehensions." Yet others felt a certain wry optimism. "Old Jack got us into this fix," muttered one marching man, "and with the blessing of God he will get us out."

Nearing Middletown, the men could hear the booming of Ewell's guns to the south and expected the worst. "The men exchanged glances," recalled one of Winder's Marylanders, "but no one spoke a word, though the same thought was in every mind, 'We are cut off now — it is all up with us.' "

Just then, a contingent of horsemen led by Turner Ashby appeared from the south, and Ashby shouted: "Is that General Winder coming up?" Told that it was, Ashby, who had ridden out from Strasburg to seek the Stonewall Brigade, breathed his bottomless relief and said: "Thank God for that!"

Shortly after noon on June 1, Jackson's old brigade staggered into Strasburg. While Ewell still faced west and dared Frémont to fight, Winder's exhausted men were given several hours to rest. Late that day, as the sun settled on the western mountains, the entire Valley army resumed its retreat.

Behind it, the turnpike began filling with frustrated Federal soldiers in pursuit.

Although Jackson had evaded the trap, his army was still in grave danger. The Union's Shields, from his position at Front Royal, could march up the Luray Valley, either crossing the Massanutten and striking Jackson's flank at New Market, or continuing south to block the Valley army's escape routes through the Blue Ridge passes. Closer at hand, Frémont, having missed his big chance, was belatedly belligerent and snapping at Jackson's rear.

Throughout the night, in a vicious storm, Jackson drove the Valley army. "The road," wrote a soldier, "was shoe-mouth deep in mud." Recalled an officer of the Stonewall Brigade: "I never saw a Brigade so completely broken down and unfitted for service."

Twelve miles south of Strasburg, the leading infantry elements overtook the tail of the supply train, and a wild tangle of men, horses and wagons brought the entire column to a halt. Jackson angrily blamed the infantry commander:

"Why do you not get your Brigade together, keep it together, and move on?"

"It's impossible, General," replied the hapless officer. "I can't do it."

"Don't say it's impossible," snapped Jackson. "Turn your command over to the next officer. If he can't do it, I'll find someone who can, if I have to take him from the ranks."

On June 3 the troops crossed the Shenandoah's North Fork, burned a bridge behind them and encamped in their old refuge on Rude's Hill near the town of Mount Jackson. After permitting a day's rest, Jackson moved on, pushing through Harrisonburg on June 5. By nightfall, the army's van was nearing Port Republic, 11 miles southeast of Harrisonburg, with the rest of the command strung out seven or eight miles behind. From a tower on the Massanutten, signal flags conveyed the welcome word that Shields's force, badly mired in the mud of the Luray Valley, was still 14 miles from Port Republic.

During the retreat, Turner Ashby had known his finest hours. Recently promoted to brigadier general, he led Jackson's rear guard in repeated, reckless charges against Frémont's pursuing Federals.

Late on the afternoon of June 6, with Jackson already halted outside Port Republic, Ashby was attacked about three miles south of Harrisonburg by Brigadier General George D. Bayard's Federal cavalry. With Ashby riding in the front rank, Confederate horsemen then sent their enemy reeling, capturing the flag of the 1st New Jersey Cavalry and taking prisoner the regiment's colonel, a colorful Englishman by the name of Percy Wyndham. "Look at Ashby," said one Confederate. "See how happy he is."

But Bayard was a dashing and aggressive commander. He had only recently recovered from an operation to remove a Commanche arrowhead embedded in his cheekbone — a wound received in prewar Indian fighting. Now, Bayard began re-forming his troopers to renew his attack. In the lull, Ashby collected two of Ewell's infantry regiments. He was guiding the 1st Maryland toward some woods, from which they could fire into the flank of the advancing Federals. Suddenly, out of those woods came a fusillade of shots from a battalion of the Pennsylvania Bucktails, Federal sharpshooters.

Ashby's horse went down. Almost in the same motion, Ashby was on his feet, waving his revolver and shouting, "Charge, men, for God's sake, charge!" A Confederate officer described what happened next: "He had not taken half a dozen steps when he fell, pierced through the body by a musket-ball, and died almost instantly. No dying words issued from his lips."

The 1st Maryland, led by Colonel Bradley Johnson, pressed its attack and carried the Federal position. But in Ashby's death the South had suffered a grievous loss.

Jackson was sitting with his staff, questioning Percy Wyndham, when he received word of Ashby's death. Jackson summarily dismissed the Englishman, saying, "I cannot see him further tonight." The general then retired to his tent to brood—and pray—in solitude. "As a partisan officer," Jackson later wrote, "I never knew his superior." For all his disciplinary shortcomings, Turner Ashby had won a permanent place in the pantheon of his homeland. "The Valley loved him," Henry Kyd Douglas wrote years later, "and loves him yet."

There was little time for mourning. With Frémont still pressing Stonewall Jackson's rear and Shields emerging from the Luray Valley, Jackson found himself between Federal forces whose courses would converge at Port Republic. As the moment of reckoning neared, Jackson put Jed Hotchkiss to

work on a detailed map of the territory.

The terrain was complicated. The little town of Port Republic lay at the end of a spit of land between the North and South Rivers, which joined just northeast of the village to form the South Fork of the Shenandoah. A single wooden bridge crossed the North River; from there, a road led northwest to Harrisonburg. Two fords—one at the northeastern edge of Port Republic and the other about a half mile farther south—offered the only passages across the South River. To

Covering their retreat up the Valley in June 1862, Jackson's troops burn a footbridge across the North Fork of the Shenandoah River, 24 miles south of Strasburg.

reach Port Republic, Shields would have to use one of the fords.

Jackson deployed most of his army along the bluffs overlooking Port Republic from the far bank of the North River. From there, his guns could sweep the town and the South River fords, thereby holding off Shields.

To block Frémont, Jackson ordered Ewell's division to deploy about seven miles southeast of Harrisonburg near the village of Cross Keys. Facing north, Ewell occupied a strong position along a ridge line — and

looked toward Frémont's arrival with relish.

Ewell would have to wait a while. Trying to induce Frémont to attack him, he maneuvered throughout the day of June 7. Frémont was also being prodded by his impulsive ally Shields, who sent a message exhorting him to "thunder down on his rear." Shields added: "I think Jackson is caught this time." Although Frémont had been bold against the Confederate cavalry, Ewell's hard-bitten infantry was another matter — and Frémont passed the day at a prudent distance.

Jackson was irritated by the Federals' failure to fight. He was also disappointed, having just learned that he would not be receiving the reinforcements he had requested. Without them he could not assume the offensive. "At present," he wrote to Richmond, "I do not see how I can do much more than rest my command and devote its time to drilling." That evening, Jackson moved his headquarters across the North River to the comforts of an estate on the western edge of Port Republic.

The 8th of June, a Sunday, was clear and cool. Early that morning, the Reverend Major Dabney asked Jackson if any military operations might be expected. "No," replied Jackson. "You know I always try to keep the Sabbath if the enemy will let me." Assuming that services would be held, Dabney returned to his cot to contemplate his sermon.

At about 9 a.m., the general and his staff were waiting for their horses to be brought around so that they could cross the North River and rejoin the army on the far bank. Just then a messenger galloped up with startling news: Federal cavalry, brushing aside a lax Confederate guard detachment, had crossed the northernmost South River ford and were entering Port Republic.

"Go back and fight them," ordered Jackson. His words were punctuated by the angry barking of musketry at the far end of town. Still afoot, Jackson started toward the sound of firing with his long, shambling stride — only to behold enemy horsemen pounding toward him down Main Street. At that instant, someone brought up the general's horse and Stonewall Jackson galloped for safety across the North River bridge.

Even as the general gained the heights, a gun was deployed at the Port Republic end of

Jackson's Confederates clash outside Harrisonburg with the 13th Pennsylvania Reserves, called the Bucktails because of the deer tails they wore on their hats. Although the Confederates drove off the Federals, their victory was a pyrrhic one — among the handful of men killed was Jackson's cavalry leader, Brigadier General Turner Ashby.

the bridge. Seeing that its crew wore blue uniforms, Jackson barked an order to his Rockbridge Artillery: "Fire on that gun!" The artillerists hesitated, protesting that the opposing gun might belong to a Confederate battery so new that its men were wearing blue uniforms. So then Jackson shouted to the men on the bridge: "Bring that gun up here!" They ignored him. Angrily, Jackson repeated his order: "Bring that gun up here, I say!" Instead, the blueclad artillerists, actually part of a Federal scouting detachment under the command of Colonel Samuel S. Carroll, began to elevate the gun — toward Jackson. Now there could no doubt. "Let 'em have it," Jackson commanded.

A brisk little artillery duel commenced. To end it, Jackson turned to Colonel Sam Fulkerson, who had hurried his 37th Virginia to the scene. Indicating the bridge and waving his cap, Jackson ordered: "Charge right through, Colonel."

Quickly clearing the bridge, Fulkerson pushed on through the town, driving out the Federals. Carroll had missed a golden opportunity — at least in the view of Shields. Had Carroll burned the bridge instead of trying to hold it, Jackson would have been highly vulnerable. As Shields wrote later: "The destruction of the bridge would have insured the destruction of Jackson's army, placing him between General Frémont and us, with an impassable river to his front."

As Jackson watched Carroll's retreat from a bluff, he exultantly raised both hands heavenward — and the men in the town below, seeing him thus silhouetted against the sky, burst into a wild cheer.

It was soon drowned out by the rumble of artillery to the northwest. John Frémont had at last decided to give battle (map, page 169).

During the skirmish at Harrisonburg, a dying Confederate color-bearer passes the 1st Maryland's flag to a comrade. In the background, on horseback, Colonel Bradley

T. Johnson urges the men on against the Pennsylvania Bucktails. At Johnson's right, Turner Ashby stands beside his dead horse; seconds later, Ashby was shot.

Advancing gingerly, Frémont's skirmishers had been held off for more than an hour by stubborn pickets of Ewell's 15th Alabama Regiment, and not until nearly 10 a.m. were Frémont's guns moved into position.

On a ridge about a mile from the Federal artillery, General Ewell was more than ready for the opening of battle. His position was ideal. A creek meandered across his immediate front. Beyond it spread several hundred acres of rolling fields that an attacking enemy would have to cross. Both of his flanks were guarded by dense woods.

Watching the Federals deploy, Ewell determined that his line was most vulnerable at its center, which was bisected by a road. There he posted four batteries, and backed them with a two-regiment infantry brigade under Brigadier General Arnold Elzey, a profane, hard-drinking veteran who had led the final Confederate charge at Bull Run. As Ewell predicted, the Federal guns did open against his center. An artillery exchange commenced, continuing until almost noon, when lines of bluecoated infantry finally began to move across the fields.

The Federal troops belonged to the division commanded by Brigadier General Louis Blenker, a German revolutionary who had emigrated to America in 1849 and later distinguished himself by covering the retreat at Bull Run. Blenker's old unit, now commanded by Hungarian-born Brigadier General Julius Stahel, was known as the German Brigade; in fact, its five regiments were a motley collection not only of Germans but of Hungarians, Italians, Swiss, Irish and American Indians.

Stahel's troops came at the Confederate right, where they were eagerly awaited by a brigade under Brigadier General Isaac R.

This photograph of Turner Ashby's corpse was taken at a farmhouse near Harrisonburg on June 6, 1862, the day he was killed by Federal troops; later the portrait was hand-tinted. Posthumous photographs were commonly produced as keepsakes for soldiers' families.

Trimble. At 60, Trimble, balding, with a full black mustache, was one of the Confederacy's oldest officers. But he remained a regular fire-eater. A West Point graduate, he had served with the U.S. Army's artillery for 10 years before resigning to become a railroad executive in Baltimore. At the outbreak of the War, he seized a train and took it northward, burning bridges to forestall the movement of Federal troops toward Washington.

Now, as Stahel's brigade advanced in parade-ground order, Trimble rode up and down his line ordering his men to hold fire until the enemy was at point-blank range.

Across the fields and up the slope came the Federals. The Confederates remained still and silent. Then at the last second Trimble gave the order, and the men rose with a shout and unleashed a solid sheet of fire. Stahel's brigade crumpled, tried to re-form and was staggered by a second volley. The men retreated in near panic, throwing Blenker's second line into confusion.

Of the 24 regiments Frémont had brought to the field, he had so far sent forward only five. Ewell expected another attack — this time in great strength. But 15 minutes passed without sign of a new assault. "They made no bayonet charge," Ewell scoffed later, "nor did they commit any particular ravages with grape or canister."

Seething with impatience, Trimble decided to go over to the offensive himself. Spying a Union battery moving into position a half mile away, he sent his men on a headlong charge to capture the guns. The Federal artillerists hastily withdrew before being overrun by the yelling Confederates.

Trimble's furious drive carried him a mile beyond Ewell's ridge — and there, daring an enemy attack, he remained all day. The Federal lassitude invited an advance of the entire Confederate line, but Ewell and Jackson, who had by now arrived at the scene, had no real choice but to remain on the defensive. Ewell's command was outmanned by about 2 to 1, and there was an ominous report of enemy movement on the Confederate left.

Late in the day, the fiery Trimble conceived the idea of a night attack. When Ewell disapproved, Trimble rode off to see Jackson, who was back in Port Republic. "Consult General Ewell," Jackson advised, "and be guided by him." But when Trimble again sought his division commander's consent to attack, Ewell shook his head and said gently: "You have done well enough for one day."

So ended the frustrating little Battle of Cross Keys. The Confederates did not come out unscathed. Two of Ewell's brigade commanders, Arnold Elzey and George H. Steuart, were badly wounded. Against Frémont's losses of 684, however, Ewell had suffered just 288. Better yet for the Confederates,

Ewell remained between Frémont and Port Republic — freeing Jackson to deal with whatever Shields might offer the next day.

To meet the Federal threat, Jackson had concocted a plan of daredevil audacity. On Monday, June 9, he meant to fight not one battle but two, first defeating Shields and then turning to finish off Frémont.

Orders were issued accordingly. Ewell would bring most of his command to Port Republic, leaving the brigades of Trimble and Colonel John M. Patton to harry Frémont at Cross Keys. Winder was told to start the Stonewall Brigade across the North River bridge into Port Republic by 4:45 a.m.

That night, Jackson flung himself onto his bed without so much as removing his boots or his sword. An hour before daybreak he was awakened by the sound of someone opening his door. "Who is that?" he called. It was Colonel John D. Imboden, one of Jackson's most trusted subordinates since the early days at Harpers Ferry. Imboden had been looking for another officer.

When Imboden tried to excuse himself, Jackson interrupted: "That is all right. It is time to be up." As the two men talked, Imboden congratulated Jackson on his victory at Cross Keys. "Yes, God blessed our army again yesterday," replied the general, "and I hope with His protection and blessing we shall do still better today."

Out before 5 a.m., Jackson met General Winder, punctual as always, leading his brigade across the North River bridge. When Winder asked for further orders, Jackson indicated only that the Stonewall Brigade should also cross the South River, on a makeshift bridge built overnight of planks laid atop supply wagons.

The Battle of Cross Keys "Sunday June 9th 1862 — E Fabes
Genl Fremont and Genl Jackson

Jackson rode with Winder across the rickety South River bridge and into the banks of fog hanging low over the bottom land of the Shenandoah. They took a road leading to the northeast and Conrad's Store — whence Shields was surely coming. The Confederate column moved silently and slowly through the gloom for about a mile. Then, at 7 a.m., a horseman brought word that there were Federals just ahead. Peering through patches of thinning fog across an expanse of ripening wheat, Jackson could glimpse the enemy in position behind a double-row fence.

Jackson was in a hurry. During the night, while giving orders to Colonel Patton, the general had vowed to dispense with Shields and return to face Frémont at Cross Keys by 10 a.m., and he intended to keep that appointment. Now, without reconnoitering or waiting for the rest of his force to come up, Jackson commanded Winder to charge.

As Federal pickets scurried back to their main line behind the fence, the Stonewall Brigade drove headlong through the waving wheat. " 'Stonewall' bore down on us like ten furies at daybreak," a Federal soldier recalled. But at that moment, a crash of Federal artillery erupted on the Confederate right, and shells scythed through the ranks of the Stonewall Brigade. Taken in flank and raked by volleys from the Federal infantry in front, the brigade faltered, stopped, fell back. "The rebels' first line was seemingly annihilated," a Federal wrote.

A disaster loomed for Jackson. As at Kernstown, he had impetuously hurled his troops into battle without proper reconnaissance; here as there, the Stonewall Brigade had rushed into an ambush set by a Federal force under the nominal command of Brigadier General James Shields. Just as at Kernstown, Shields himself was absent from the field. This time he was to the rear at Conrad's Store, having just arrived from Luray with two brigades. Jackson faced Shields's vanguard: two brigades, totaling 3,000 men, under Brigadier General Erastus B. Tyler, a 40-year-old Ohioan.

Jackson had little time to ponder tactics. Seeking the source of the enemy artillery fire, he saw to his right a foothill of the Blue Ridge stretching toward the battlefield. Midway up the spur was a "coaling," a flat clearing where wood was burned for charcoal. From that coaling, seven concealed Federal guns — three of them long-range Parrott rifles — poured down their deadly fire on the Stonewall Brigade.

If the brigade were to survive, the coaling must be taken, and quickly. At Jackson's command, Winder sent the 2nd and 4th Virginia Regiments off to the right and into the mountainside wilderness. A Confederate battery, instructed to follow, gave up the attempt after its guns became hopelessly entangled in dense undergrowth.

The infantry regiments fared little better. Climbing, chopping and cursing their way through wild thickets of mountain laurel, they finally reached a point about 100 yards from the enemy guns. Then, to their considerable consternation, they found the guns supported by three regiments of Federal infantry. A Confederate volley drove the Federal artillerists from the coaling, but the gunners returned under covering fire from their own infantry. Swinging their guns around, they blasted the Confederate attackers with canister. The Confederates retired — and the murderous Federal fire was resumed against the Stonewall Brigade on the plain below.

The failure to seize the coaling convinced Jackson that he could no longer hope for a double victory on that day. He sent word for Trimble to withdraw from Frémont's front, hasten across the North River bridge and burn it so as to keep the Pathfinder at bay. Then Trimble was to cross the South River and rush to the battle. That movement, however, would require far more time than Jackson could presently afford. The Stonewall Brigade, pinned down and hanging on for its life, needed help immediately.

And help, as luck would have it, was on the way. Double-timing up the road from Port Republic came Colonel Harry T. Hays's 7th Louisiana Regiment of Taylor's Brigade. Like the rest of Richard Taylor's command, Hays had been held up by the improvised bridge across the South River, so shaky by now that it could only bear the weight of men passing over it in single file.

Jackson instantly sent Hays to bolster Winder's wavering line. Then he could only wait for more reinforcements; with face downturned and with reins resting on his horse's neck, he appeared to one officer as if he were praying for reinforcements. Up cantered Taylor, cool and collected, with the rest of his brigade. Jackson's greeting was laconic: "Delightful excitement." Pointing to the smoke belching from the enemy guns on the mountainside, Jackson turned to Jed Hotchkiss: "Take General Taylor around and take those batteries." Into the thickets went Hotchkiss and Taylor.

Meanwhile, the Federals opposite Winder were plainly preparing to charge and add their weight to the galling artillery fire. Winder calculated that the Stonewall Brigade could not possibly withstand such an onslaught, and he decided to strike first.

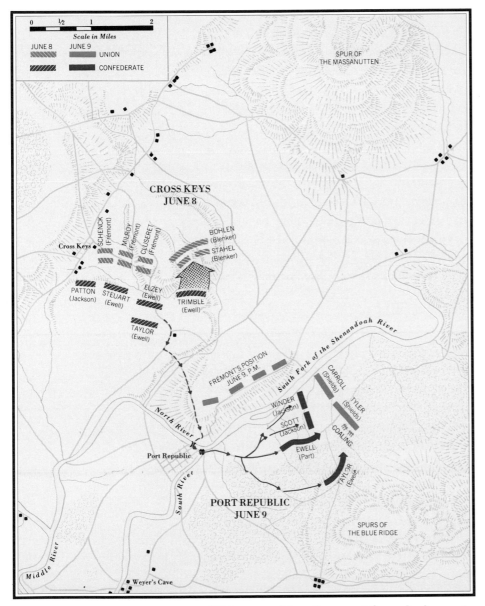

SPUR OF
THE MASSANUTTEN

CROSS KEYS
JUNE 8

Cross Keys

SCHENCK
(Frémont)

MILROY
(Frémont)

CLUSERET
(Frémont)

BOHLEN
(Blenker)

STAHEL
(Blenker)

PATTON
(Jackson)

STEUART
(Ewell)

ELZEY
(Ewell)

TRIMBLE
(Ewell)

TAYLOR
(Ewell)

FRÉMONT'S POSITION
JUNE 9, P.M.

South Fork of the Shenandoah River

North River

WINDER
(Jackson)

SCOTT
(Jackson)

CARROLL
(Shields)

TYLER
(Shields)

COALING

EWELL
(Part)

TAYLOR
(Ewell)

Port Republic

South River

PORT REPUBLIC
JUNE 9

SPURS OF
THE BLUE RIDGE

Middle River

Weyer's Cave

On June 8, Stonewall Jackson halted Frémont's advance in the hills just east of Cross Keys. That night, Jackson boldly shifted the bulk of his forces across the North River and on the morning of June 9 attacked James Shields northeast of Port Republic, forcing him to withdraw. Frémont, who had resumed his advance, was stymied when Jackson burned the North River bridge.

Seeing their enemy pinned down, the Federals redoubled their fire across the fence. Decimated, the Stonewall Brigade broke, first in a trickle and then in a flood, with Winder and his staff frantically trying to stop the rout.

Just when the Confederates seemed about to collapse, Richard Ewell arrived at the battlefield and sized up the grim situation with a soldierly eye. He immediately ordered two of his regiments — the 44th and 58th Virginia — to fall on the left flank of the advancing enemy.

The startled Federals fell back. Still, they were ably commanded and well in hand; quickly recovering, they wheeled left and drove Ewell's force into the mountainous forest beneath the coaling. Ewell made the best of a bad situation. On horseback he led his men up the mountain to try to take the troublesome Federal guns.

By then, Taylor badly needed whatever aid he could get. Masked by heavy timber and undergrowth, he had struggled to a position near the coaling. "The head of my column began to deploy," recalled Taylor, "when the sounds of battle to our rear appeared to recede, and a loud Federal cheer was heard, proving Jackson to be hard pressed."

Although his deployment was not yet completed, Taylor ordered a charge. "With a rush and shout," he wrote later, "we were in the battery. Surprise had aided us, but the enemy's infantry rallied in a moment and drove us out." Taylor and his men clawed back. This time the Federal gunners fought hand to hand, using their rammers as clubs. Again, the Federal infantry rallied and Taylor was repulsed. For the third time, he gathered his force and charged, with even the

Without waiting for word from Jackson, he ordered a charge.

Across the wheat field swept the Stonewall Brigade, with Hays and his Louisianians on its right. They reached the fence at the edge of the field, but there, faced by a point-blank blaze of musketry, the brigade was forced to the ground. Already, the men were running low on ammunition.

169

drummer boys joining the brawl. At last, Taylor possessed the coaling.

Or did he? Up the mountainside forged Erastus Tyler and three of his Ohio regiments. "With colors advanced, like a solid wall he marched straight upon us," wrote Taylor. "There seemed nothing left but to set our backs to the mountain and die hard."

Just as it appeared that Taylor would surely be overwhelmed, Richard Ewell and his men came crashing out of the wilderness and into the clearing. Now faced with superior numbers, Tyler retreated to rejoin Shields's main force. The coaling belonged to the Confederates. Now the guns were turned to pour fire against Shields's men on the open plain beside the river. Ewell himself delightedly manned one of the cannon.

At about the same time, more Confederate reinforcements, including William Taliaferro's brigade, arrived from Port Republic and streamed onto the plain. Slowly, reluctantly, the Union's forces turned and began leaving the field, moving northward in good order. They had done all that they could—and it had very nearly been enough.

As the sound of firing faded, Jackson encountered Ewell. "General," he said, "he who does not see the hand of God in this is blind, sir, blind."

In the close-fought and, for Jackson, poorly managed Battle of Port Republic, the Valley army suffered 615 casualties, its greatest losses of the campaign. That the Union lost 1,018 men, including 558 captured, was no compensation to Jackson's small army. As a Confederate officer conceded, "It is but bare justice to say that the enemy on this field fought stubbornly and well."

After the battle, John C. Frémont advanced to the bluffs overlooking the battlefield from the far side of the river and lobbed a few shells into a Confederate ambulance park. He then withdrew to Harrisonburg, and thence to Mount Jackson, while Shields retreated to Luray.

As for Jackson, he moved to a strong position at Brown's Gap in the Blue Ridge and awaited the next enemy move. But after a few days passed without threat, he descended again into the Valley, establishing his headquarters near Weyer's Cave on a road from Port Republic to Staunton. And there Jackson's Valley Campaign came to a quiet close.

During the past 10 weeks Jackson had made mistakes even by standards less rigorous than his own. Yet he had more than fulfilled his mission. Perhaps the most perceptive analysis of the campaign had already come from the opposite camp. Shortly after Irvin McDowell's movement toward Richmond had been suspended, the Federal general remarked to a fellow officer, "If the enemy can succeed so readily in disconcerting all our plans by alarming us first at one point, then at another, he will paralyze a large force with a very small one."

On June 14, from the camp near Weyer's Cave, Thomas Jonathan Jackson wrote to his wife, who was staying in Richmond. The letter ended wistfully: "Wouldn't you like to get home again?"

That was not to be. On June 17, 1862, Jackson left the Shenandoah Valley forever. He was heading toward Richmond— where Robert E. Lee, granted time by the Valley Campaign, was preparing to attack George McClellan.

A portrait of Stonewall Jackson painted by a Confederate soldier depicts the general as he appeared during the Valley Campaign. Of Jackson, General Richard Taylor wrote: "Praying and fighting appeared to be his idea of the 'whole duty of man.' What limit to set on his ability I know not, for he was ever superior to occasion."

ACKNOWLEDGMENTS

The editors thank the following individuals and institutions for their help in the preparation of this volume:
Louisiana: New Orleans — Charles Dufour; William Menary, Howard Tilton Memorial Library, Tulane University.
Maryland: Clinton — William Turner.
New York: Jamestown — Ellen Fessenden, Fenton Historical Society.
Virginia: Alexandria — Susan Cumbey, Wanda Dowell, Fort Ward Museum and Park; Sandra S. O'Keefe, Allan Robbins, Alexandria Library, Lloyd House. Front Royal — Alma Noland, Lola Wood, Warren Rifles Confederate Museum. Lexington — Barbara Crawford, Michael Lynn, Stonewall Jackson House; June F. Cunningham, Virginia Military Institute Museum. McLean — Virginia Nelson. New Market — Robert Myers, New Market Battlefield Park. Richmond — Rosemary Arneson, Virginia State Library; Cathy Carlson, David Hahn, Museum of the Confederacy; Elizabeth Childs, Sarah Shields, Valentine Museum. Staunton — Hanna Bush, Stonewall Brigade Band; Frank B. Holt. Winchester — H. Robert Edwards; Elaine Hall, Winchester-Frederick County Historical Society.
Washington, D.C.: Barbara Burger and Staff, National Archives, Still Picture Branch; Jim Flatness, Library of Congress, Map Division; Maja Felaco, Jerry L. Kearns, Library of Congress, Prints and Photographs Division.
West Virginia: South Charleston — Terry Lowry.
France: Paris — Claude Bellarbre, Marjolaine Matikhine, Musée de la Marine.
The index for this book was prepared by Nicholas J. Anthony.

PICTURE CREDITS

Credits from left to right are separated by semicolons, from top to bottom by dashes.

Cover: Painting by John Adams Elder, courtesy Confederate Memorial Hall, photographed by Bill van Calsem. 2, 3: Maps by Peter McGinn. 8-17: Prints by Edward Beyer, courtesy Virginia State Library. 19: National Portrait Gallery, Smithsonian Institution, Washington, D.C. 20, 21: Library of Congress. 23: Stonewall Jackson's Headquarters Museum/Winchester-Frederick County Historical Society, photographed by Larry Sherer, except left, New Market Battlefield Park, Hall of Valor Museum, photographed by Larry Sherer. 24: Courtesy Historic Lexington Foundation, Stonewall Jackson House, photographed by Larry Sherer. 26, 27: Painting by James Walker, courtesy Department of Defense, inset, courtesy Historic Lexington Foundation, Stonewall Jackson House, photographed by Larry Sherer. 30-32: Virginia Military Institute Museum, photographed by Larry Sherer. 34: Courtesy Historic Lexington Foundation, Stonewall Jackson House. 36, 37: National Archives Neg. No. 79-CWC-3F2. 39: Print by W. L. Sheppard, courtesy Museum of the Confederacy. 41-43: Courtesy Frank & Marie-T. Wood Print Collections, Alexandria, Virginia. 45: Museum of the Confederacy, photographed by Larry Sherer. 47: Courtesy Historic Lexington Foundation, Stonewall Jackson House. 48, 49: Courtesy Frank & Marie-T. Wood Print Collections, Alexandria, Virginia. 50: Valentine Museum, Richmond, Virginia. 51: Museum of the Confederacy, courtesy Historical Times Inc. 53: Museum of the Confederacy. 54: Courtesy Mark Katz, Americana Image Gallery. 56: Museum of the Confederacy, photographed by Larry Sherer. 57: Courtesy J. Craig Nannos, photographed by Larry Sherer, except top right, courtesy Don Troiani, photographed by Henry Groskinsky. 60-63: U.S. Army Military History Institute, copied by Robert Walch. 64, 65: Courtesy Frank & Marie-T. Wood Print Collections, Alexandria, Virginia. 66: Map by Walter W. Roberts. 68, 69: Courtesy Frank & Marie-T. Wood Print Collections, Alexandria, Virginia. 70: National Archives Neg. No. 111-BA-1568. 72-81: West Virginia Department of Culture and History. 83: Museum of the Confederacy, photographed by Larry Sherer. 84, 85: From *Stonewall Jackson's Way* by John W. Wayland, The McClure Co., Inc., Staunton, Virginia, 1940; Library of Congress Map Division, photographed by Jeffrey Wilkes (2) — Stonewall Jackson's Headquarters Museum/Winchester-Frederick County Historical Society, photographed by Larry Sherer (3). 88, 89: Courtesy Frank & Marie-T. Wood Print Collections, Alexandria, Virginia. 90, 91: From *Stonewall Jackson's Way* by John W. Wayland, The McClure Co., Inc., Staunton, Virginia, 1940; Stonewall Jackson's Headquarters Museum/Winchester-Frederick County Historical Society, photographed by Larry Sherer — courtesy heirs of Jack Ashby Moncure and Mildred Wright Moncure, photographed by Larry Sherer — Museum of the Confederacy, photographed by Larry Sherer (2) — Stonewall Jackson's Headquarters Museum/Winchester-Frederick County Historical Society, photographed by Larry Sherer. 93: Courtesy Bill Turner, copied by Henry Beville. 95: Library of Congress. 96, 97: Painting by Charles Hoffbauer, courtesy Virginia Historical Society, photographed by Henry Groskinsky. 98: From *Battles and Leaders of the Civil War: Grant-Lee Edition*, published by The Century Co., New York, 1884-1887. 100: Library of Congress. 101: Map by Walter W. Roberts. 102: Special Collections, Tulane University Library. 105, 106: Courtesy Bill Turner, copied by Henry Beville. 107: Virginia Military Institute Museum, copied by Larry Sherer. 108-110: Courtesy Bill Turner, copied by Henry Beville. 111: Virginia Military Institute Museum, copied by Larry Sherer. 112, 113: Courtesy Bill Turner, copied by Henry Beville. 115: Virginia Military Institute Museum, photographed by Larry Sherer. 116: From *Gentle Tiger: The Gallant Life of Roberdeau Wheat* by Charles L. Dufour, Louisiana State University Press, Baton Rouge, 1957. 117: From *Battles and Leaders of the Civil War: Grant-Lee Edition,* published by The Century Co., New York, 1884-1887. 118, 119: Painting by Johannes A. Oertel, courtesy Fenton Historical Society, Jamestown, New York, photographed by Lon Mattoon. 120: Special Collections, Tulane University Library. 122: Warren Rifles Confederate Museum, Front Royal, Virginia, copied by Larry Sherer. 124, 125: Photo Bulloz, from *Le Monde Illustré,* courtesy Musée de la Marine, Paris. 126, 127: Courtesy Warren Rifles Confederate Museum, Front Royal, Virginia, photographed by Larry Sherer. 130: Map by Walter W. Roberts. 131: Courtesy Frank & Marie-T. Wood Print Collections, Alexandria, Virginia. 132: Courtesy Frank B. Holt. 134, 135: Painting by William D. Washington, courtesy Valentine Museum, Richmond, Virginia, photographed by Larry Sherer. 136, 137: Library of Congress. 138, 139: Western Reserve Historical Society, inset, Library of Congress. 140, 141: National Archives Neg. No. 111-B-383. 142, 143: From *Russell's Civil War Photographs: 116 Historic Prints* by Andrew J. Russell, Dover Publications, Inc., New York, 1982. 144, 145: Library of Congress. 147: Virginia Military Institute Museum, photographed by Larry Sherer. 148: State Historical Society of Missouri. 150: Courtesy Frank & Marie-T. Wood Print Collections, Alexandria, Virginia, 152, 153: Library of Congress. 154: U.S. Army Military History Institute, copied by Robert Walch; Library of Congress (2). 155: Courtesy Brian Pohanka; courtesy Michael J. McAfee. 158-161: Courtesy Frank & Marie-T. Wood Print Collections, Alexandria, Virginia. 162, 163: Library of Congress. 164: Stonewall Jackson's Headquarters Museum/Winchester-Frederick County Historical Society, copied by Larry Sherer. 166, 167: Library of Congress. 169: Map by Walter W. Roberts. 171: John Adams Elder: *General Thomas Jonathan Jackson,* in the Collection of The Corcoran Gallery of Art, Gift of William Wilson Corcoran.

BIBLIOGRAPHY

Books

Allan, William, *History of the Campaign of Gen. T. J. (Stonewall) Jackson in the Shenandoah Valley of Virginia.* Press of Morningside Bookshop, 1974.

Ballard, Colin R., *The Military Genius of Abraham Lincoln.* The World Publishing Company, 1952.

Bean, W. G., *Stonewall's Man: Sandie Pendleton.* University of North Carolina Press, 1959.

Beyer, Edward, *Album of Virginia; or Illustration of the Old Dominion.* Virginia State Library, 1980.

Black, Robert C., III, *The Railroads of the Confederacy.* University of North Carolina Press, 1952.

Boatner, Mark Mayo, III, *The Civil War Dictionary.* David McKay Company, Inc., 1959.

Bowman, John S., ed., *The Civil War Almanac.* World Almanac Publications, 1983.

Boyd, Belle, *Belle Boyd in Camp and Prison.* Ed. by Curtis Carroll Davis. Thomas Yoseloff, 1968.

Brice, Marshall Moore, *The Stonewall Brigade Band.* McClure Printing Company, Inc., 1967.

Bushong, Millard K., *General Turner Ashby and Stonewall's Valley Campaign.* McClure Printing Company, Inc., 1980.

Casler, John O., *Four Years in the Stonewall Brigade.* Press of Morningside Bookshop, 1981.

Catton, Bruce, *This Hallowed Ground: The Story of the Union Side of the Civil War.* Doubleday & Company, Inc., 1956.

Chambers, Lenoir:
Stonewall Jackson, Vols. 1 and 2. William Morrow & Co., 1959.
Stonewall Jackson and the Virginia Military Institute: The Lexington Years. Garland Gray Memorial Research Center, 1959.

Cohen, Stan, *The Civil War in West Virginia: A Pictorial History.* Pictorial Histories Publishing Company, 1982.

Commager, Henry Steele, ed., *The Blue and the Gray*, Vol. 1. The Bobbs-Merrill Company, 1973.

Cook, Roy Bird, *The Family and Early Life of Stonewall Jackson.* Education Foundation, Inc., 1967.

Cooling, Benjamin Franklin, *Symbol, Sword, and Shield: Defending Washington during the Civil War.* Archon Books, 1975.

Couper, William, *History of the Shenandoah Valley*, Vol. 2. Lewis Historical Publishing Company, Inc., 1952.

Crute, Joseph H., Jr., *Confederate Staff Officers, 1861-1865.* Derwent Books, 1982.

Curry, Richard Orr, *A House Divided: A Study of Statehood Politics and the Copperhead Movement in West Virginia.* University of Pittsburgh Press, 1964.

Dabney, R. L., *Life and Campaigns of Lieut.-Gen. Thomas J. Jackson.* Blelock & Co., 1866.

Davis, Burke, *Jeb Stuart: The Last Cavalier.* Rinehart & Company, Inc., 1957.

Davis, William C., ed., *The Guns of '62 (The Image of War: 1861-1865*, Vol. 2). Doubleday & Company, Inc., 1982.

Douglas, Henry Kyd, *I Rode with Stonewall.* University of North Carolina Press, 1940.

Dufour, Charles L.:
Gentle Tiger: The Gallant Life of Roberdeau Wheat. Louisiana State University Press, 1957.
Nine Men in Gray. Doubleday & Company, Inc., 1963.

Dwight, Wilder, *Life and Letters of Wilder Dwight.* Ticknor and Fields, 1868.

Egan, Ferol, *Frémont: Explorer for a Restless Nation.* Doubleday & Company, Inc., 1977.

Ewell, Richard S., *The Making of a Soldier: Letters of General R. S. Ewell.* Ed. by Percy Gatling Hamlin. Whittet & Shepperson, 1935.

Foote, Shelby, *The Civil War, a Narrative: Fort Sumter to Perryville.* Random House, 1958.

Freeman, Douglas Southall:
Lee's Lieutenants: A Study in Command, Vol. 1. Charles Scribner's Sons, 1942.
R. E. Lee: A Biography, Vol. 2. Charles Scribner's Sons, 1934.

Gordon, George H., *Brook Farm to Cedar Mountain in the War of the Great Rebellion, 1861-62.* James R. Osgood and Company, 1883.

Gordon, John B., *Reminiscences of the Civil War.* Charles Scribner's Sons, 1903.

Hamlin, Percy Gatling, *"Old Bald Head" (General R. S. Ewell): The Portrait of a Soldier.* Shenandoah Publishing House, Inc., 1940.

Harrington, Fred Harvey, *Fighting Politician: Major General N. P. Banks.* University of Pennsylvania Press, 1948.

Henderson, G.F.R., *Stonewall Jackson and the American Civil War*, Vols. 1 and 2. Longmans, Green, and Co., 1909.

Hotchkiss, Jedediah, *Make Me a Map of the Valley: The Civil War Journal of Stonewall Jackson's Topographer.* Ed. by Archie P. McDonald. Southern Methodist University Press, 1973.

Hungerford, Edward, *The Story of the Baltimore & Ohio Railroad, 1827-1927.* G. P. Putnam's Sons, 1928.

Jackson, Mary Anna, *Life and Letters of General Thomas J. Jackson.* Harper & Brothers, 1891.

Jacob, Diane B., and Judith Moreland Arnold, *A Virginia Military Institute Album, 1839-1910.* University Press of Virginia, 1982.

Johnson, Robert Underwood, and Clarence Clough Buel, eds., *Battles and Leaders of the Civil War*, Vol. 2. Thomas Yoseloff, Inc., 1956.

Johnston, Angus James, II, *Virginia Railroads in the Civil War.* University of North Carolina Press, 1961.

Jones, J. B., *A Rebel War Clerk's Diary at the Confederate States Capital*, Vols. 1 and 2. J. B. Lippincott, 1866.

Lee, Robert E., *The Wartime Papers of R. E. Lee.* Ed. by Clifford Dowdey. Bramhall House, 1961.

Lonn, Ella, *Foreigners in the Union Army and Navy.* Greenwood Press, 1951.

McDonald, Cornelia, *A Diary, with Reminiscences of the War and Refugee Life in the Shenandoah Valley: 1860-1865.* Cullom & Ghertner Co., 1934.

McDonald, William N., *A History of the Laurel Brigade.* Ed. by Bushrod C. Washington. R. W. Beatty, Ltd., 1969.

McWhiney, Grady, and Perry D. Jamieson, *Attack and Die: Civil War Military Tactics and the Southern Heritage.* University of Alabama Press, 1982.

Nevins, Allan:
Frémont: Pathmarker of the West. Frederick Ungar Publishing Co., 1955.
The Improvised War, 1861-1862. (The War for the Union, Vol. 1). Charles Scribner's Sons, 1959.

Nicolay, John G., *A Short Life of Abraham Lincoln.* The Century Co., 1904.

O'Ferrall, Charles T., *Forty Years of Active Service.* The Neale Publishing Company, 1904.

Opie, John N., *A Rebel Cavalryman with Lee, Stuart and Jackson.* Press of Morningside Bookshop, 1972.

Paxton, Frank, *The Civil War Letters of General Frank "Bull" Paxton, C.S.A., a Lieutenant of Lee & Jackson.* Ed. by John Gallatin Paxton. Hill Jr. College Press, 1978.

Poague, William Thomas, *Gunner with Stonewall.* Ed. by Monroe F. Cockrell. McCowat-Mercer Press, Inc., 1957.

Robertson, James I., Jr., *The Stonewall Brigade.* Louisiana State University Press, 1963.

Sandburg, Carl:
Abraham Lincoln: The Prairie Years. Harcourt, Brace and Company, 1926.
Abraham Lincoln: The War Years, Vol. 1. Harcourt, Brace & World, Inc., 1939.

Saunier, Joseph A., ed., *A History of the Forty-Seventh Regiment Ohio Veteran Volunteer Infantry, Second Brigade, Second Division, Fifteenth Army Corps, Army of the Tennessee.* Lyle Printing Co., 1903.

Sigaud, Louis A., *Belle Boyd: Confederate Spy.* The Dietz Press, Incorporated, 1944.

Smith, Elmer Lewis, John G. Stewart and M. Ellsworth Kyger, *The Pennsylvania Germans of the Shenandoah Valley.* The Pennsylvania German Folklore Society, 1964.

Stutler, Boyd B., *West Virginia in the Civil War.* Education Foundation, Inc., 1963.

Summers, Festus P., *The Baltimore and Ohio in the Civil War.* G. P. Putnam's Sons, 1939.

Tanner, Robert G., *Stonewall in the Valley.* Doubleday & Company, Inc., 1976.

Taylor, Richard, *Destruction and Reconstruction: Personal Experiences of the Late War.* D. Appleton and Company, 1879.

Thomas, Benjamin P., and Harold M. Hyman, *Stanton: The Life and Times of Lincoln's Secretary of War.* Alfred A. Knopf, 1962.

Thomason, John W., Jr., *Jeb Stuart.* Charles Scribner's Sons, 1930.

United States War Department, *The War of the Rebellion: A Compilation of the Official Records of the Union and Confederate Armies.* Government Printing Office, 1902.

Vandiver, Frank E., *Mighty Stonewall.* McGraw-Hill Book Company, Inc., 1957.

Warner, Ezra J., *Generals in Blue: Lives of the Union Commanders.* Louisiana State University Press, 1964.

Wayland, John W.:
Stonewall Jackson's Way. The McClure Company, Inc., 1940.
Twenty-Five Chapters on the Shenandoah Valley. C. J. Carrier Company, 1976.

Williams, Kenneth P., *Lincoln Finds a General: A Military Study of the Civil War*, Vol. 1. The Macmillan Company, 1949.

Williams, T. Harry, *Lincoln and His Generals.* Vintage Books, 1952.

Worsham, John H., *One of Jackson's Foot Cavalry.* Ed. by James I. Robertson Jr. McCowat-Mercer Press, Inc., 1964.

Other Sources

Hassler, William W., "Dr. Hunter Holmes McGuire: Surgeon to Stonewall Jackson, the Confederacy, and the Nation." *Virginia Cavalcade*, Autumn 1982.

Holt, Frank B., "Stonewall Brigade Band: Continuous Since 1855." Unpublished paper, Staunton, Virginia.

Johnson, Bradley T., "Memoir of the First Maryland Regiment: The Affair at Sangster's Station." *Southern Historical Society Papers*, Krauss Reprint Co., 1977.

"Stonewall in the Shenandoah: The Valley Campaign of 1862." *Civil War Times Illustrated*, May 1972.

Wright, R. Lewis, "Edward Beyer in America: A German Painter Looks at Virginia." *Art & Antiques*, November/December 1980.

INDEX

Time-Life Books Inc. offers a wide range of fine recordings, including a *Big Bands* series. For subscription information, call 1-800-621-7026, or write TIME-LIFE MUSIC, Time & Life Building, Chicago, Illinois 60611.